The
UNSEEN POWER
of
PRAYER
A CATHOLIC PERSPECTIVE

Also by Michael McDevitt:

Alive with the Life of Christ:
Prayers for the Ordinary Circumstances of Life

The Parish Leadership Team Plan: A Step-by-Step Guide
to a Whole Community Parish Retreat
(updated annually)

The Eucharist and the Mystical Humanity of Christ
Rob Bussell, Ph.D., and Michael McDevitt
(A series of retreat booklets for reflection)

A Day with Jesus and His Mother
(DVD story of a highly successful parish retreat)

For more information, please visit *www.ParishRetreat.org*
or e-mail *mysticalhumanity@aol.com.*

The UNSEEN POWER *of* PRAYER

A CATHOLIC PERSPECTIVE

MICHAEL McDEVITT

Our Sunday Visitor Publishing Division
Our Sunday Visitor, Inc.
Huntington, Indiana 46750

Nihil Obstat: Rev. Michael Heintz, Ph.D.
Censor Librorum

Imprimatur: ✠ John M. D'Arcy
Bishop of Fort Wayne-South Bend
August 9, 2008

The *Nihil Obstat* and *Imprimatur* are official declarations that a book or pamphlet is free of doctrinal or moral error. No implication is contained therein that those who have granted the *Nihil Obstat* or *Imprimatur* agree with the contents, opinions, or statements expressed.

To Pam:
"I love you through Christ."

"This experience is a new concept for me — one that all Catholics should be exposed to. This form of prayer makes it a comfortable and memorable communication with Jesus."

RETREAT PARTICIPANT

Author's Note

Throughout this book, I have included quotes from people who have participated in our retreats. These comments personalize the "power of prayer" for people living with a heightened awareness of the presence of Jesus in their daily lives.

Contents

Acknowledgments

⸺

During my life, I have received many blessings. To acknowledge every person who has influenced my thinking is an impossible task. I do wish to express appreciation to Father Vito Perrone, Father Jim Hanley, S.J., and my cousins Father Bob McDevitt, S.J., Mary Jean DuPont, and Michael Huston, people of unwavering faith and dependability; Rob Bussell, Ph.D., a great pal who consistently demonstrates the meaning of faith that is alive; Mary Beth and Bill O'Connell, and Gina and Al Barber — couples who are "friends forever"; and the late Bob Holstein, who was by my side from our days at Loyola High School until his sudden death in January 2003.

Bob exemplified what it means to be a person of faith, and many of my characteristics have been modeled after his example.

I received the greatest of blessings when I met Pamela Kirkpatrick on a blind date. I know Our Lord blessed us and our marriage from day one. I love her and thank God for her. Family is everything, and my children, sons-in-law, and grandchildren are a true reflection of people who love one another. I owe a special acknowledgement to my daughter, Lisa Cost, for her many hours proofreading and editing the manuscript.

FATHER FRANK

I have wonderful memories as a young boy growing up. Often on a Sunday evening, an uncle, Father Frank Parrish, S.J. (1911-2003), would come to our house for dinner with four or five of his Jesuit brothers. The house was filled with the sounds of debate and laughter and music. It was the custom that after dinner we would all gather in the living room where one priest would play the piano and the rest of us would sing. Occasionally, my father, Dr. John McDevitt, would play the violin. It was during these childhood years that I met Cora Evans. She was a family friend, and Father Frank was her spiritual director. Her writings changed my life, and I am eternally grateful for the choices she made in her life. The family gatherings were always joyous events; and although some of the participants have passed on to their eternal reward, I am sure their joy continues.

I have been greatly influenced by the Jesuits, having experienced their companionship and friendship. I have seen them relaxed, having fun, and in serious debate. I was educated by

Jesuits and predisposed to the teachings of St. Ignatius of Loyola from the time I was five years old. I am especially indebted to Father Frank for being a constant source of inspiration. He opened my eyes to the magnificent love Jesus has for me personally, a love He has for each one of us. Father Frank passed away on December 29, 2003, but his message is always with me.

MY MOTHER AND FATHER

I owe my faith to my mom. I was nine years old when my father became physically disabled. Mom did it all. She played the dual role of mother and father. She was a stay-at-home mom who decided to start up a business and run it from the home long before people considered such decisions feasible. She was an inspiration to everyone who knew her, and to others who have heard her story of faith, hope, and joy.

My disabled father had halting speech and difficulty communicating. Nonetheless, he set an example of living what had to be monotonous days in the context of faith. He never missed Sunday Mass, and during Lent the parish priest brought Communion to him daily. As a boy growing up, I learned that the words of faith are not as inspiring as the *witness* of faith.

The late Dick Huston, husband of my cousin Mary Joyce Roletti Huston, befriended my father with many visits and became my mentor. He was like a second father to me. On parting, Dick would always say, "Keep the faith." Today, his son Michael works with me facilitating retreats.

CHRISTIAN FRIENDS

Many of my friends are Christians of different denominations — not Catholic. The Jesus they love is the Jesus I love, and He loves each of us with 100 percent of His love. Perhaps we are like the debaters who argue one side of the argument or the other. After the debate, they go out to dinner, break bread, and enjoy the companionship. I simply ask my Christian friends to look to the common love we have for the person in Whom our faith is based. Our differences will be resolved in time. For now, know that I love, bless, and appreciate you.

CORA EVANS

For over 10 years, I have resisted talking about Cora Evans, much less writing about her. But things have changed and the devotion to the Indwelling — the Mystical Humanity of Christ — is rapidly spreading as a way of prayer. Now is the appropriate time.

I was a student at Loyola High School in Los Angeles when I read *The Refugee from Heaven*, Cora's full-length book recounting the life of Christ. That first book led to reading everything of Cora's I could get my hands on. This unique opportunity, reading the works of a Catholic mystic, was possible because of the role of Father Frank, who was her spiritual director, and my mother, who retyped many of Cora's manuscripts.

Over the years, I would ask Father Frank what he intended to do with Cora's writings. He didn't have an answer. His primary role in the life of this great mystic was to provide spiritual guidance and direction.

When she died in 1957, his guiding role in her life was complete. The question of the disposition of her writings remained unanswered for 35 years. Perhaps it is the "squeaky wheel" syndrome (I'm not sure), but in 1992 Father Frank asked me to be the custodian of the writings and mission of Cora Evans. I immediately said "Yes!" Then, after a long pause, I asked a question: "What's a custodian?"

Over the next few months, Father Frank provided clear direction, and we agreed that the role of custodian included the proper disposition of her writings and the continuation of her mission to promote the Mystical Humanity of Christ — the indwelling presence of Jesus. We agreed that the process established by the Catholic Church* to investigate causes of sanctity must be followed.

Cora resided in Boulder Creek, California, when she died. Therefore, it is the Diocese of Monterey where the review commenced. In March 1995, Most Reverend Sylvester D. Ryan, D.D., then bishop of the Diocese of Monterey, appointed a committee composed of the diocesan judicial vicar and two parish priests. Their task is to review the writings of Cora Evans and submit a formal report. Most Reverend Richard Garcia, D.D., was installed as bishop of Monterey on January 30, 2007. Once the work is completed, her writings will be forwarded to the Vatican for the comprehensive review. In the meantime, selected writings of Cora Evans are being published to generate greater awareness of the Mystical Humanity of Christ throughout the world.

GETTING STARTED

It was a Sunday afternoon when Mark Montgomery called to say he won an automobile in a fund-raising drawing the night

---

* Causes of this nature are governed by the norms of Pope John Paul II's 1983 apostolic constitution *Divinus Perfectionis Magister* and the particular procedural law of the Congregation for the Causes of Saints.

before. He accepted the cash award rather than the vehicle. Then he announced that he was splitting the money between Thomas Aquinas College and our new nonprofit organization, the Mystical Humanity of Christ, Inc. With their donation, Mark and Irene Montgomery became our first benefactors. A few months later I had what turned out to be a five-hour lunch with June MacMurray.* She decided to provide a level of consistent financial support that would ensure the continuation of this new ministry. June had a special relationship with Father Frank. Besides being a close friend, he had been her spiritual adviser.

The financial support of these three people made it possible for us to launch the organization. June had known Cora Evans — they were personal friends — and she reminded me that Cora did not ask to be a mystic, Father Frank did not ask to be her spiritual director, and I did not ask to be custodian. She spoke of the spirituality of fund-raising. We all have a role to play, she said, and each one is being asked to do his or her part. I owe a special "thank you" to Mark and Irene Montgomery and June Haver MacMurray.

The promulgation of the Mystical Humanity of Christ is now my life's work. Cora encourages us to strive for the knowledge of the Indwelling:

> [Having] Christ within us is to know that our five senses
> have been crucified and died [and] that we are nothing
> but a cocoon emptied of self. And the life put into that
> cocoon is Jesus Himself[,] Who in turn continues reliv-

---

* June Haver MacMurray (1926-2005) appeared in fourteen major motion pictures. She was married to the actor Fred MacMurray (1908-1991).

ing His life of the resurrection through us. Through our eyes He sees, through our ears He listens and through our footsteps He travels and blesses. We are His portable tabernacles! What a mission in life!

The purpose of this book is to spread an awareness of the Indwelling — the Mystical Humanity of Christ. I take no credit for fresh ideas presented here. My understanding of the Mystical Humanity of Christ, the name itself, was attained through the writings of Cora Evans and the illuminations shared by Father Frank.

Introduction

I can recall precise times in my life when I prayed. The prayers were event driven — a response to circumstances beyond my control, times when I needed help from God. Today my way of prayer is a daily connection, a continuous dialogue with Jesus. I don't wait for the event.

Through Baptism, we share a common grace and the same vocation to perfection, the same destiny to become saints. St. Ignatius of Loyola defines this grace as the divine life dwelling within us. The idea behind this book is to create a heightened awareness of the living, indwelling presence of Jesus in the lives of the faithful. By sharing certain aspects of my personal faith journey, I reveal the move from event-driven prayer to the richness of daily prayer.

The first chapter is about embracing the mystery of faith. A person of faith is one who integrates his or her spiritual life with every other aspect of life.

Chapter Two encourages you to reflect on the indwelling Spirit of God and recommends how to make this your way of prayer every day. In the process, you become alive with the life of Christ.

In Chapter Three, I share my personal experience of reconciliation and how the experience shed light on this extraordinary gift from God.

The fourth chapter addresses the question of how to participate in the perfect prayer, the Mass. Praying the Mass is the centerpiece, the place where we find the fullness of the power of prayer. In the Eucharist, we have the life of the Creator, Who desires that we allow His mission to continue through us.

In Chapter Five, I share my past struggle with Mary and what I learned about her intimate connection with the Eucharist. The role of Joseph, guardian of the Holy Family, provides us with a unique personality to identify with in meditative prayer.

In Chapter Six, I teach by example, by sharing my dialogue with Jesus.

The discovery of the unity we share through prayer is featured in Chapter Seven.

Even though Chapter Eight, on trusting Jesus, is the shortest, it asks the one question you must be prepared to answer.

Chapter Nine, "Encourage Others," includes a selection of letters written to a young man with cancer. At times, we unknowingly become the instrument Our Lord uses in responding to the prayers of another person. Here is an example of how anyone may be called to play an indispensable role in the unseen power of prayer.

The final chapter, "Pray Always," is about your choices and the role Jesus is entrusting to you personally.

MY FIRST CONVERSATION WITH JESUS

My earliest recollection of praying happened when I was nine years old. My story begins when I was goofing around while waiting in line with my third-grade friends at Holy Family Elementary School in South Pasadena, California. Recess was over and Sister Dolorenda, in her frightening black-and-white nun's habit, stormed up to our group, and in a loud voice shouted, "Michael McDevitt, your father is in the hospital dying, and you're standing here goofing around in line!"

An etching was made in my memory. I can see her, and hear her, even now. My friends all turned to me and asked, "Is your dad dying?" I knew my dad had not been home because he was ill, but no one had ever said anything like that.

I don't recall how I answered my friends. But I do know that later that day I ran home to find out. Third-graders aren't supposed to leave school in the middle of the day, but that didn't stop me.

As it turned out, my father did not die. When he came home from the hospital, however, he was an invalid, paralyzed on the right side. The brain surgery left him unable to speak. One day he left home for work as a highly successful physician, and as chief of staff at Queen of Angels Hospital in Los Angeles. When he arrived home 17 days later, his life had forever changed. Mine, too.

I could write a book about my mother and how she supported the family by creating a home-based business before people did such things. And how we never missed Sunday Mass. And how, together, my parents became a living example of faith for everyone they encountered.

It is all part of my heritage. As an adult reflecting on heritage, I now realize the tremendous value given to me by the two most influential people in my life.

BARGAINING WITH GOD

No one else was present when I entered Holy Family Church in the afternoon. During mid-week, it always seemed that I had the whole church to myself. I knelt at the communion rail, right in the middle, so that I could look directly at the tabernacle. My dialogue went something like this: "Dear Jesus, if you make my daddy better, I'll help Mommy with the dishes every night this week."

The following week, having received all the brownie points possible for helping with the dishes, I was back at the communion rail. I knew that God heard my first prayer, but maybe I needed to up the ante. My new prayer expanded the offer: "Dear Jesus, not only will I help with the dishes, but I'll clean my room every day!"

Nothing changed at home. Dad learned to walk with a cane. His bedroom, where he spent most of his time, looked like a first-grade classroom, with large letters of the alphabet posted on the walls, typical school posters, and other school supplies. My dad, a highly educated physician, was relearning how to speak. He would never practice medicine again. Somewhere along the way, my bargaining with God stopped. Some might conclude that my prayers were not answered, that God could not be dealt with by bargaining — and who was my dad, anyway, to be entitled to such a miracle?

THE POWER OF PRAYER

I believe that every prayer is answered with a blessing. Every time I prayed for my father, he received Our Lord's blessing. Perhaps he received the grace to help him on his most difficult days, times when he felt lost and alone. I don't know. But I reflect on my actions when I was a nine-year-old with a sense of appreciation for the graces my father received. My dad was never able to play sports with me, but few people learn the example of faith and courage he taught me — not by what he said, because he couldn't talk in complete sentences, but by his very life.

I was with him 16 years later when he died. Our family was gathered around his bedside. We were aware that these were his final moments, and I lifted the oxygen mask off his face. Almost as if on cue, Dad lifted the crucifix he held in his hand up to his lips and kissed it. A second time he lifted it, trying to kiss it one more time, but he took his last breath in the process. Imagine dying while trying to kiss the crucifix.

A lot of people prayed for my father over the years. As a child, I prayed for a miracle. All of those prayers were answered in God's own special way in the end.

EVENT-DRIVEN DIALOGUE PRAYER

There are events in life that compel us to turn to God. Even if a person has been away from active participation in the life of the Church for years, a crisis forces them to their knees. It is a bow to the supremacy of God and a belief in the power of prayer.

Many events have driven me to pray in particular ways. As a child, I tried to bargain with God. I prayed for discernment at a major turning point in my life. In the midst of turmoil, I expressed anger with God, then pleaded for help. I turned to Jesus and asked for His help dealing with the sudden death of a friend. Even as a child, I treated God as someone Who listened, a person with Whom I had an ongoing relationship, a friend.

Engaging in prayer with a sense of faith and hope is not something foreign. I believe it is the grace of Baptism that draws us into conversation with Jesus. When I needed discernment, my prayer was a conversation with Jesus that laid everything on the table. So much was at stake that I could not imagine the consequences of making the wrong decision.

DISCERNMENT

As a young man, I was accepted into the diaconate program for the Diocese of San Francisco. The diaconate is the only ordained ministry for married men in the Catholic Church. The deacon receives the Sacrament of Holy Orders, the same sacrament conferred on priests, without the privilege to say Mass or hear confessions. Deacons support their parish by presiding over and blessing marriages, baptizing, proclaiming the Gospel and preaching, presiding over funerals, and many other ministries. It was a three-year program of classes in theology, Scripture, the sacraments, and the doctrine of the Catholic Church. It included many weekend events — social gatherings, studying, and retreats — and often included the wives of the candidates. We had three young children at the time, and I was one of the youngest in the class.

As we got closer to the ordination date, we were asked to write a white paper about how we intended to respond to God's calling. What did I want to do as a deacon? The more I thought about it, the less it seemed that I truly had a vocation. I wrote about starting a program designed to help troubled youth. The program would be affiliated with the Partners program in Denver. It was a Big Brothers/Big Sisters type of matchup, but set apart because of the willingness of adult volunteers to match up one-on-one with kids who were defined as delinquent or at risk.

As I thought about this new role, it became clear that I did not see myself in the traditional role of a deacon. While preaching seemed a natural, the baptizing and performing marriage ceremonies did not seem to fit. With only a few months to go before ordination, I was faced with the most fearful decision of my life. For three years, I had moved toward becoming a deacon. The decision to apply, the hours of study, the shared decisions with my spouse — everything felt like it was coming to a head. My biggest fear was that if I resigned from the program, I would be turning my back on something God wanted me to do. Would I be rejecting a vocation?

In the depths of my soul, I struggled with these thoughts. I was not at peace about the ordination, nor did I feel any sense of peace about resigning. I prayed for discernment.

MY DECISION

My last class in the program was held on a Thursday evening at St. Patrick's Seminary in Menlo Park. A visiting priest gave a lecture based on the book *As Bread That Is Broken*, by Peter G. van Breemen, S.J., a Dutch priest. His lecture featured the love of God for each one of us, and he said: "God loves you with 100 percent of His love. You don't get 110 percent if you do one thing and only 90 percent if you do another." Bam! That lightning bolt struck me as though his whole lecture had been designed to answer my prayer for discernment. I thought to myself, "You mean, I could resign from the program, and God will still love me with 100 percent of His love?"

It was the permission I needed. Within a few days, I wrote my letter of resignation. For the first time in months, I felt at peace. There has never been a single moment since that time that I looked back with regret. That's what happens with discernment. The true measure is the sense of peace. Had I made another decision, I would not have felt at peace.

Today I have the benefit of three years of study at St. Patrick's Seminary with some of the best theologians and professors around. It has given me a solid education for my ministry. And I am certain of one thing in particular: God loves you with 100 percent of His love. It is a message for us all.

DAILY PRAYER

There will always be events that compel us to turn to God. This book is about building the relationship so that when the time comes, you are not like the stranger asking for a favor. It is about acknowledging that Jesus wishes to play a role in your life every day. He awaits your invitation.

THE UNSEEN POWER

The power of prayer is not about your power, but the power you have allowed inside — Christ Himself is the unseen power. You are fused with a power far beyond anything you can imagine. St. Paul urges us to live by this faith: "We look not to the things that are seen but to the things that are unseen; for the things that are seen are transient, but the things that are unseen are eternal" (2 Cor 4:18).

Jesus is that unseen fire deep within your soul. But you must fan the flame, or else it will become a tiny spark with no warmth to share.

CHAPTER ONE

Embrace the Mystery of Faith

"This form of prayer is at the center of our Christian faith. In essence, my motivation becomes His motivation; my word, His word; my desire, His desire! I really appreciate your emphasis on this today. We need more teachings in our Church on this form of prayer — praying in the heart — centering on the Holy Spirit within."

RETREAT PARTICIPANT

On the inside of my wedding band are initials that translate to "I love you through Christ," a slogan Pam and I developed when we were engaged. Our relationship is grounded in our faith. Jesus is the third partner in our marriage, the glue that binds us together.

THE ONE CHALICE

Before launching on a new career move that would be a full-time ministry for me and 100 percent commitment for her, we took a walk around the Crystal Springs reservoir near our home. The ministry is the promotion of the indwelling presence of Jesus, the Mystical Humanity of Christ, as a way of prayer life for Catholics. We concluded that this was a single blessing between our third partner and ourselves. It was not given as a separate blessing to me and a separate blessing for Pam. We are spiritually united in the reception of this extraordinary gift.

We reflected on the question Jesus asked the mother of Zebedee's sons. She asked Jesus for a favor: "Command that these two sons of mine may sit, one at your right hand and one at your left, in your kingdom." Jesus responded with a question to her two sons: "Are you able to drink the chalice that I am to drink?" (Mt 20:21, 22). Pam and I thought about the new ministry as the chalice we were being offered. He was asking us the same question. There are not two separate chalices, one for Pam and the other for me.

As we reflected on Jesus' question, we realized that whatever our roles in life, we can elect to accept the chalice Jesus gives us. We can place everything before Him and offer it to Him as our prayer and our way of being aware of the complete integration of Jesus into our everyday lives. This is what loving each other through Christ means. We imagined Jesus drinking from a chalice and then offering it to us. Will we tell Jesus that we are not thirsty? Will we say we are not ready? Or will we sip from the chalice and then raise it up and offer a toast in His honor?

During our walk, we more fully understood the chalice offered at the Last Supper and the meaning of His words:

And he took a chalice, and when he had given thanks he said, "Take this, and divide it among yourselves. . . . This chalice which is poured out for you is the new covenant in my blood." (Lk 22:17, 20)

Jesus is the life within the chalice that is poured out for us to drink. When we accept the chalice, we accept Jesus. By positioning our ministry in the context of His chalice, we accept Jesus.

We were anxious because of the unknown. This would not be an easy path. But it would be a cakewalk compared to the chalice Jesus accepted. In the Garden of Gethsemane, Jesus fell to the ground, exhausted, in prayer: "My Father, if it be possible, let this chalice pass from me" (Mt 26:39). This sentence gives us insight into the depth of the love Jesus has for us. His chalice includes all the times it is offered and rejected. He is shattered by the defiance and rejection of the friends who disown Him. At the same time, His chalice includes all the saints and sinners of the world who have accepted it and loved Him for it. It is so far beyond the individual chalice offered to one person that it is immeasurable.

In the garden, we hear the anxiety in the voice of Christ. In the fullness of His humanity, He wonders if He can pass the chalice to someone else. And then He expresses His love for us in the most profound way: "Not my will, but yours, be done" (Lk 22:42). He turns Himself over to the will of the Father. He accepts the chalice.

Jesus is offering us the chalice. For Pam and me, our "yes" came with no strings attached. We were being offered the only drink that can quench a spiritual thirst.

Faith is about accepting the chalice Jesus offers you. Many have dared to drink from it. Many have passed. Today the chalice is being offered again, and Jesus is asking you: "Will you drink of the chalice?"

TRUTHS TO PONDER

Questions raised in private by retreat participants often reflect universal questions in the hearts of others. What would Jesus propose for me to do? How does a silent God speak? How do I become a person of prayer? How can I forgive and forget? How do I keep my faith alive? There are many questions, and even more truths, to ponder. What I have learned is that Jesus is present in your life, right now.

Any desire on your part to be drawn to a closer, more intimate relationship with Jesus was placed there by Him as His gift to you. Although your life is hectic, you are being called out of that hecticness to focus once more on the spiritual connection you have with Our Lord. It is the same spiritual connection you have with others. The voice you hear today is calling you to become more aware of the living, indwelling presence of Jesus. The questions become: Will you invite Him? What will He find in the temple that is you? Will you allow Him to bless others, speak to others, and touch others through you?

The Second Vatican Council, in its treatise on the Church, explains the mandate given to lay people in carrying out the divine plan of Jesus for the salvation of souls:

> Each individual layman must stand before the world as a witness to the resurrection and life of the Lord Jesus and a symbol of the living God. (*Lumen Gentium*, Dogmatic Constitution on the Church [November 21, 1964], n. 38)

The council emphasizes the way of divine love in everyday life:

> To those, therefore, who believe in divine love, He gives assurance that the way of love lies open to men and that the effort to establish a universal brotherhood is not a hopeless one. He cautions them at the same time that this charity is not something to be reserved for important matters, but must be pursued chiefly in the ordinary circumstances of life. (*Gaudium et Spes*, Pastoral Constitution on the Church in the Modern World [December 7, 1965], n. 38)

It is with this backdrop that *The Unseen Power of Prayer* was written. Pray that you are awakened to His indwelling within you, and that you will recognize His presence in others.

AWAKEN

It seems that we are always in a hurry to get someplace which is more important than where we are right now. We don't have time to stop because something "over there" is more important than the place we occupy. As we develop a deeper relationship with Jesus, we become alert to His indwelling presence, which exists only in the present moment. It is not about arriving at a new destination where we will realize a new level of awareness; it is about being awake now, fully alive with the life of Christ today, and confident there is more to come.

Often questions are posed from the restless hearts of people not satisfied that they are doing enough or that they are worthy of the mission entrusted to them. Two things matter when reflecting on these questions:

"Jesus was present. I felt his love and gift of peace. I was blessed to share this special day with so many wonderful people. Jesus was the face of everyone who attended."

RETREAT PARTICIPANT

- First, develop a deeper relationship with Jesus. I recommend practicing dialogue prayer because it opens you to experiencing His personal love for you. Drop all the concerns about worthiness and accept the truth that Jesus already decided that you are worth it. God's will for you becomes apparent when you express your love in return for the love Jesus gives to you. Never forget that doing God's will is not about doing something to earn God's love; it is about doing something that shows gratitude. For me, writing this book is my gratitude in action.

- Second, there is no such thing as the people who are called and those who are not called. Having read that last sentence, there is no turning back. There is no opportunity to step aside. Jesus has, quite literally, a burning desire to have a personal relationship with you.

NEVER BECOME COMPLACENT

There are Catholics — friends and family members, people I know personally — who appear to drift away at times. Perhaps they are still searching for something. Hopefully, they have not become so assured of God's love that they have become complacent. The unintended result of complacency is that it insults Jesus.

The impact of the broken Body of Christ is incalculable. When you leave the Church, I am diminished. I am the Body of Christ — not by myself, but with you. There is great rejoicing when a baptized Catholic returns.

Recently, I discussed my ministry with a close personal friend. I used the DVD-formatted presentation that I show to Church leaders. Our 15-minute movie was edited down from 10 hours of video shot at a highly successful parish retreat. It tells our story from the perspective of parishioners who attended one of our parish events. My friend's first comment was, "I wonder why I don't feel the way you feel?" In other words, why isn't his faith leading him to do more?

"I've been reluctant to even consider Jesus in my life for the past 13 years. It has been a desert time for me. God has been calling me back, and it has been hard for me to accept myself. Through your sharing and the sharing of the groups, God has broken through the walls and begun the healing process. Spending a Saturday sharing time with people I do not normally associate with and truly searching to strengthen my association with Jesus was <u>not</u> a top priority. I was surprisingly wrong! It was amazing how, at the end of the day, you felt a common bond or closeness to the others in the room; although strangers, they felt like family because we were one in Christ. This retreat was excellent for me. Thank you.

"PS: I'm glad my wife made me come."

RETREAT PARTICIPANT

I responded by talking about my unique upbringing with an uncle, a Jesuit priest, who was the spiritual director for a mystic, and about the exposure I had to the mystic's writings and eventually being asked to be the custodian of her writings. "But you still made the decision to do what you're doing, and you have zeal about your faith that I don't have" was his response.

Over the next few days, I found myself reflecting on his question, "Why don't I feel the way you feel?" It is the perfect question for those who want their faith to come alive. The answer is found in the field of psychology, not religion. Feelings follow behavior. The feelings of faith follow the behavior of faith; it is not the other way around. The inactive Catholic will not suddenly "feel" differently simply by the desire for different feelings. A change in behavior comes first. In order to "feel" differently, the inactive Catholic must make a different choice than the one being made.

Each of us has the ability to choose to pray, to ask God for help. It is always our choice. Our Lord is a patient Lord. His love is unchanging; it is being given to you at this moment regardless of the choice you make. Becoming alive with the life of Christ is a choice. It is about dialogue prayer becoming a way of life. It is about committing yourself to a heightened awareness of the constant presence of God in your life. It is not about waiting for the right *feeling*.

If you have been away for a while, you will find encouragement by reading Luke 15:11-32. It is the great story of the joy of reconciliation.

MY BEST FRIEND DIED

Bob Holstein was my best friend, going back to our days at Loyola High School. As adults we enjoyed reminiscing about the stories of our rowdy behavior, the pranks, and the escapes and close calls. I recall many conversations while sitting in the hot tub at his home in Riverside. That's where I developed a critical part of my social conscience. Before long, our conversations would drift to meaningful subjects, and my strong-willed friend would challenge my thinking on subjects ranging from liberation theology to the "real" issues in some remote Third World country.

When the subject of Bob Holstein comes up among friends and acquaintances, the conversation quickly centers on his involvement in social justice. He wasn't just the one who crossed the line in protest against the School of the Americas at Fort Benning, Georgia; he recruited you to do the same. It wasn't enough to stand up for what he believed; he went to jail for civil disobedience. He didn't just ask you to support a cause; he set the example by creating an endowment. Many people have labeled him a social activist, but that description falls short.

Bob's death was sudden. He went to the hospital one afternoon for what should have been a routine procedure. He died because of medical maltreatment. Regardless of the emotions his treatment conjures up, the fact remains the same: Bob died. Nothing ever hit me so hard. My father's death was expected. Other family members and the deaths of friends were either anticipated or somehow more acceptable. This was not the case with Bob. It was an abrupt ending. It felt cruel and harsh. How would Loretta, his wife, cope? His children needed him. What about all the causes he supported? Who could possibly replace Bob Holstein? But something even more unsettling was going on. In the depths of my soul, a piece of me was missing.

My tears of sorrow were for me, my loss. Later, reflecting on our relationship and my feelings in particular, I kept coming back to the realization that my best friend experienced something that I had not experienced. He took that final step in life. He knows what that experience is like. I don't. I have to wait. And now I pray about it. I imagine Our Lord sitting at the kitchen table across from me. We are engaged in conversation, and some of the old stories come up — the ones about rowdy behavior, the pranks, the fun-loving stories with my pal Bob. And then things get serious. And Jesus asks about my faith. He wants to know how I have used my gifts, the special ones He gave me, and who has benefited from them.

The reflection, sitting at the kitchen table with Jesus, has become an important and frequent way of prayer. Bob taught me something else about prayer. Bob did what he did in the context of faith. It was his relationship with Jesus Christ that motivated him. Faith was always the underpinning of his actions. For me, the walk-away result is the desire to do what I do in the context of faith. Just like Bob.

THE INSEPARABILITY OF FAITH

A person of faith is one who integrates his or her spiritual life with every other aspect of life. Although the spiritual life is distinguishable from the material life, the two seem inseparable to a person of faith, because, in fact, they are inseparable. There is no moment when one is present to the exclusion of the other. When deep in meditative prayer, we are still material beings aware of our surroundings. When attending a sporting event, we are still spiritual beings as well. We cannot simply check our spirit at the door. The challenge is to be aware of the integration and to live accordingly.

A person of faith not only begins the day with prayer but has the opportunity to invite Jesus to be a part of every moment of the day that is about to unfold. From time to time during that day, this faithful person will ask Jesus to bless those who have crossed his or her path. Some days will go by with no recollection of Jesus at all, and yet this person knows that Jesus was there, fully present, fully aware. Reflection at the end of the day will bring about laughter and satisfaction, or embarrassment and shame, and the resolution to do better the next day.

RECONNECT NOW

Many inactive Catholic bystanders hope for a renewed sense of direction, a way to reconnect. We all can agree that St. Peter was a person of faith. Jesus asked Peter, "Do you love me?" Peter responded, "Yes, Lord; you know that I love you." To Peter's surprise, Jesus repeated the question, "Do you love me?" (see Lk 21:15-19). Apparently, Jesus was not satisfied with Peter's answer.

In the silence of your soul, the temple in which God dwells, Jesus is asking you the same question. What answer do you give? What is it about your answer that is believable, more believable than Peter's answer, so that Jesus doesn't have to repeat the question? There will be a day when you will meet Jesus face-to-face. If you become alive with the indwelling life of Christ now, His voice will sound familiar. You will have anticipated His question. Now is the time to rehearse your answer.

CHAPTER TWO

Become Alive With the Life of Christ

"The Mystical Humanity of Christ is not simply a concept but a reality for everyone who professes that Christ is Our Lord, Our Redeemer. The blessing was a beautiful way of helping our family to know they are strengthened by their received grace. And this morning, as I began my new job as principal of a big middle school, I know Christ was in me, acting in me, and coming to all the people I met today! Thank you, and God's blessings on your continued, needed work!"

RETREAT PARTICIPANT

I'm going to live forever. I may spend 100 years here on earth, but how can that compare to my first 100 billion years in heaven? The reason why this insight is important is that the manner in which I spend the 100 billion hinges on how I spend the 100 years. There is a simple understanding about life that forms the basis for a discussion of the unseen power of prayer: your eternal life has already begun. You don't live one life here on earth that is disconnected from your life after death.

EMBRACE A RADICAL IDEA

If you choose to accept this teaching, it will change your life. The challenge is to breathe life to a radical idea: the Spirit of God dwells in you — you are a dwelling place for Jesus. St. Paul posed the idea as a question to the Christian community in Corinth, "Do you not know that you are God's temple and that God's Spirit dwells in you?" He continued: "For God's temple is holy, and that temple you are" (1 Cor 3:16, 17).

The Divine Indwelling may be the least understood idea in all of Christianity. It was beautifully articulated by St. Paul, it is the centerpiece of the Gospel of John, and many saints have written about it, yet it often remains omitted from daily prayer and, consequently, out of the reach of Christians who lack awareness and understanding.

The Cross of the Resurrection* is the symbol that awakens us to an awareness of what we already know, of what exists but is not yet fully realized. For Christians, this cross represents an acknowledgment of our communion with one another. Jesus, the resurrected Christ, is counting on your help. You are being asked to serve as never before. Jesus is asking you for permission to allow Him to use you to spread His love every day with every person you encounter. When you understand His request, you will have awakened to the Divine Indwelling. When you accept it, you will be living with an awareness of the unity of your spirit with the Spirit of Jesus. This idea helps us understand the meaning of grace, which St. Ignatius of Loyola defined as "simply God's life, the divine life in us." The cross serves to remind us of this sacred connection.

---

* The Cross of the Resurrection does not bear a corpus, an image of the crucified Jesus. It is a plain cross with a robe draped over the cross beam. This cross symbolizes both the act of redemption and the Resurrection.

BECOME ALIVE WITH THE LIFE OF CHRIST

Like the flame of two candles coming together, the Divine Indwelling is the personal presence of the Spirit of Jesus Christ united with your spirit. St. Thérèse of Lisieux, "The Little Flower," expressed her desire with a prayer: "I want Jesus so to draw me into the flames of His love, so to make me one with Himself that He may live and act in me." This is about the living soul of Jesus united with your soul. It is not intended to be some passive presence of God — or to acknowledge that God is everywhere, and that this must include being within you. The Indwelling is about the active presence of Jesus, and it calls you to a heightened awareness of His life within you.

Blessed Mother Teresa posed a rhetorical question: "Am I truly united to Jesus as I should be, so that I can say with St. Paul, 'I live, it is no longer I that live but Christ who lives in me'?" (private audience lecture, San Francisco, June 4, 1982). You are called to make a decision. Your decision can only be yes or no — there is no room for equivocation. You cannot avoid making a choice. In the end, you will either respond to this teaching or choose not to listen to the inner voice you hear. It is the choice between complacency and renewal, between indifference and rebirth. If you choose not to respond, Jesus will find those who will.

One of the characteristic themes of Christianity is that of an inner revolution and continuous spiritual rebirth. This rebirth is a higher life in Christ. The intention here is not to explain a radical idea, but to lead you to a new way of life, living daily with the indwelling Spirit in mind. Cora Evans encourages us to better understand the Indwelling: "Through us He uses our bodies to accomplish His works of mercy and love. *We are His holy dwelling places*. Let us strive for greater perfections in the knowledge of the Indwelling."

Cora's mission in life was to lay the groundwork for the promulgation of the Mystical Humanity of Christ throughout the world. The sole purpose of this form of prayer is to develop a deeper and more active relationship with Jesus in a way that transforms your life. What an extraordinary opportunity. What power you have. Imagine a world in which all people are aware of the Divine Indwelling — the Mystical Humanity of Christ. This is the awareness Jesus is leading us to.

THE MYSTICAL HUMANITY OF CHRIST

In the Gospel according to John, we read the last discourse of Jesus:

> "Yet a little while, and the world will see me no more, but you will see me; because I live, you will live also. In that day you will know that I am in my Father, and you in me, and I in you." (Jn 14:19-20)

Father Frank said it this way:

> I've always been of the mind that the Mystical Humanity of Christ was the life of the interior Indwelling of God's Holy Spirit. That Christ, the blessed Trinity itself, *dwells within us*. It's that we become His other humanity, His resurrected life. He died and left the world, true, but He continues to live in His resurrected life through our humanities. To me this is the very heart and apex of our Catholic faith. It is a devotion which is strength-

ened by the Eucharist, the cornerstone of our faith. (Stated during an interview with the author, November 1992)

This teaching is reinforced by the first encyclical of Pope Benedict XVI: "God incarnate draws us all to himself. We can thus understand how *agape* also became a term for the Eucharist: there God's own *agape* comes to us bodily, in order to continue his work in us and through us" (*Deus Caritas Est*, On Christian Love [December 25, 2005], n. 14). Jesus made a promise when He said, "I will not leave you desolate; I will come to you" (Jn 14:18). He keeps His promises.

SACRAMENTAL AND SPIRITUAL COMMUNION

The Eucharist is the deepest and most profound gift God has given to mankind, which is why it is referred to as "Holy Communion." St. John Vianney (1786-1859), the patron saint of parish priests, said: "A spiritual communion acts on the soul as blowing does on a cinder-covered fire which is about to go out. Whenever you feel your love of God growing cold, quickly make a spiritual communion."*

The Mystical Humanity of Christ is a way of daily prayer. It is not a substitute for the Eucharist, nor does it in any way replace the Eucharist. The Mystical Humanity is the Indwelling. You are putting on Christ. You enthusiastically declare with St. Paul, "Christ lives in me!" By extending the invitation to Jesus, you are reminded that you have become His

---

* The saint, known as the Curé (parish priest) of Ars, became pastor of Ars, France. He was canonized in 1925, and his feast day is August 4.

hands, His voice, and His eyes throughout the day. As such, this practice is truly a way of life. When you are unable to attend Mass and receive Holy Communion, make a *spiritual communion* (see Pope John Paul II's encyclical *Ecclesia de Eucharistia*, On the Eucharist in its Relationship to the Church [April 17, 2003], chapters 4 [n. 34] and 6 [n. 56]). Empty yourself of self and invite Jesus to dwell within you.

There is a symbiotic relationship between the Eucharist and the Mystical Humanity of Christ. The Mystical Humanity draws you to the Eucharist; the Eucharist draws you to the Mystical Humanity. When you commit to this form of prayer, Jesus becomes the prevailing theme of your life.

The birth of Jesus was a single point in history. It happened once. It will not happen again. The work of the Incarnation, however, which began at His birth and continued throughout His life, is not complete. The mission of Christ did not end on Good Friday. It continues today, and the role you play is essential to its continuation. Jesus is calling His followers to become more than goodwill ambassadors. In a society that tells you to strive for everything, Jesus is asking you to surrender yourself. Only by surrendering do you make room for Jesus to live within you.

There is no half-measure in your devotion to Jesus in His Mystical Humanity. It is a complete surrender to Our Lord — every day. You begin the day by extending an invitation to Jesus to live His resurrected life through you. The light of Christ, His Light, flows through you to every person you encounter. You are charged with spreading the Gospel, and this renewed focus on your relationship with Jesus is a daily reminder of what God is accomplishing through you.

BECOME AN ICON OF JESUS

St. Paul tells us that God's love has been poured into our hearts through the Holy Spirit. When you invite Jesus to live His resurrected life through you, you identify with the words of Paul and live with a heightened awareness of His presence. With your simple prayer, you have become an icon of Jesus. It is at once a beautiful and scary thought. The beauty is in knowing that you are actually taking Jesus with you, and that He is blessing others through you. The fear is that you will stumble or fall; that you will expose your invited guest to the darkness of your worst behavior. And yet, the good far outweighs the bad. You willingly run the risk because you know that even at your worst you will quickly seek reconciliation. You move forward boldly with the knowledge that this is what Our Lord wants you to do.

Today you must make yourself aware of the presence of Jesus in your life, no matter how busy your schedule or conflicted you have become with worldly stress and pressures. It is precisely because of these tensions that you must bring Jesus with you. You need Him. The world needs Him. Perhaps you will be the one person who takes Him into the coldest worldly situation that can only be survived with His warmth. On that day, you are the vehicle through which Jesus realizes His plan. Begin your day with Jesus in the Eucharist. Continue your day with His Mystical Humanity. Become alive with the life of Christ.

PERSONAL EXPERIENCE OF PRAYER

Can anyone promise that if you pray a certain way, your prayers will be answered just the way you requested? There are as many ways to pray as there are ways to say "I love you" or "Thank you" or "Help" or "Wow." How, then, should we pray? There is no one way. Allow me to share my personal experience of prayer.

My first moment of prayer arrives when I become aware of being in the presence of God. It is like acknowledging someone in a room just before you approach that person to engage in a conversation. It is an awareness of a pending moment of encounter.

The second moment of prayer happens when I initiate the conversation with Jesus. This all takes place in my thoughts, yet there is a real presence that is felt and a real conversation that takes place. I don't *pretend* as though I'm communicating with someone; I am communicating. The conversation has consistency from day to day, in that there is sameness to my greeting:

> Jesus, I love You, and I believe You are truly here present with me. I begin my prayer by asking for Your forgiveness of all my sins. Trusting in having received that forgiveness, I empty myself of self; I surrender myself to You, and invite You to relive Your resurrected life, Your Mystical Humanity, through me today.

The first sentence conveys my feelings and absolute certainty of His presence. The second sentence recognizes the faults of my human nature, for which I am forever sorry. It reminds me that I have hurt a friend. Jesus has already forgiven me, but it helps put me in the right frame of mind. The next sentence begins with an act of faith: trusting in having received forgiveness. For me, however, the last part is the core prayer of my life: I invite Jesus to dwell within me. This is the indelible mark of my faith. I believe the invitation is accepted again and again, each and every day.

SACRED TIME

Intellectually, I am quite certain that Our Lord knows every petition in my heart. Nevertheless, it seems my prayers include petitions: to make this situation better, to help me resolve the problem. The list goes on and on. Gradually, I am learning to trust and eliminate the requests. When I do that, I reap the benefits of peace and joy that are found in quiet prayer. Quiet prayer is just what the words imply: there is no sound, just awareness. This is sacred time, and there are no requests for favors. There exist only reflections, listening, feelings, and inspirations.

Quiet time of prayer begins with a sense of calm. I've placed myself in the presence of Jesus. I allow my mind to take a stroll and ponder the vast mysteries of God. This quiet time is a source of inspiration and enlightenment about the things I should do: activities that I believe are God's will, and guidance about how to accomplish them. Prayer leads to doing things: engaging in good works or social action; writing about Jesus; talking and teaching about Jesus; leading others to find Jesus. Principally, prayer is about finding Jesus and sharing the discovery.

There is always a prayer of thanksgiving for the blessings I receive through others. There is always the prayer of hope for people who are trying to discover their true self, and connect with the Holy Spirit of Jesus Who is within them.

I believe in the unseen power of prayer and the reality of prayer. There is no more powerful connection than the spiritual attachment to Christ that comes through prayer. As a retreat leader, I have been asked by many retreatants to pray for their special intentions. Conversion and physical healing are the two most frequent requests. Often it is for family members who have willingly left the Catholic Church.

When you tell someone that you will pray for them, it is essential that you keep your promise. We are connected spiritually through Christ, and we must not allow the words "I'll keep you in my prayers" to become a trite phrase, with the same meaning as "Have a nice day." When you offer to pray for someone, you have made a holy promise. Our Lord expects you to keep it. Better not to promise than not to keep the promise.

How should you pray? What are the words of prayer? The answer is found when you pray. It is not about using the correct formula. It is about opening the lines of communication between you and Jesus. It does not take someone else to tell you how. All it takes is faith.

THE BLESSING

Typically, on our retreats we bless each other by making the Sign of the Cross on the recipient's forehead while we say this prayer from Cora Evans: "May God bless you with all the desires of the eternal Father, and bless the wishes of your soul, in the name of the Father, and of the Son, and of the Holy Spirit. Amen."

The prayer calls upon Our Lord to respond to the wishes of the person being blessed, and it is said in the context of God's will for that person. You pray for God's blessing, and the person for whom you are praying receives this unseen power. It is a pure prayer that places absolute trust in Our Lord. When you bless your children and your loved ones in this way, they receive something miraculous: a grace from God. As the person giving the blessing, you are fully aware of the presence of Christ within you. Although it is not in Scripture, it is not difficult to imagine Jesus saying, "Bless one another as I have blessed you."

"To receive a blessing is nourishing, but to give it? I began feeling unworthy, and then felt blessed that another person trusted me enough to receive Christ through me."

RETREAT PARTICIPANT

AWAKEN, CHILDREN OF LIGHT

Many people consider St. Paul's Letter to the Ephesians, written from his prison cell, to be the most spiritual of New Testament thought. In chapter 5, we have Paul's famous passage that views Christians as children of light and quotes poetry to symbolize our passage from lack of faith to being awakened:

> For once you were darkness, but now you are light in the Lord; walk as children of light (for the fruit of light is found in all that is good and right and true), and try to learn what is pleasing to the Lord. Take no part in the unfruitful works of darkness, but instead expose them. For it is a shame even to speak of the things that they do in secret; but when anything is exposed by the light it becomes visible, for anything that becomes visible is light. Therefore it is said,
>
> "Awake, O sleeper, and arise from the dead,
>   and Christ shall give you light." (Eph 5:8-14)

The Light of Christ penetrates your very being. This Light is not a symbol, but rather His actual presence. He is not calling you to ordinary prayer; He is calling you to actually become one with Him. This is not about some future event; it is not the result of a good life or something to be achieved when you die. The Light, His Light, is present now.

Recently, I gave a talk, "The Power of Prayer," with my friend, Cyndi Peterson, M.D. She shared her remarkable journey of faith and how one family survived the deaths of two children, with a stronger faith than before those tragic events took place. She lives in the Diocese of San Diego and is married to an orthopedic physician. They have three young boys at home and two daughters in heaven. Cyndi has been featured on EWTN, Ave Maria Radio, and has spoken at conferences nationwide.

I asked Cyndi how she keeps track of all the people who approach her for prayers. She told me that whenever someone asks for prayers, she places that person in her heart. When she says her prayers, she asks Our Lord to bless them all. She spoke of uniting her heart with the Sacred Heart of Jesus and the Immaculate Heart of Mary. It reminded me of the prayer Father Frank would say at every Mass. He asked Jesus to bless all those who had asked him for prayers. Like Cyndi and Father Frank, we can place people in our hearts and ask Jesus to remember them all.

CHAPTER THREE

＝

Pray for Reconciliation

"Forgiveness is a wonderful gift from God. I can't think of anything that compares to the feeling of being at peace with God — knowing that my sins are forgiven and forgotten."

RETREAT PARTICIPANT

The purpose of prayer and its value hinge on understanding reconciliation. This is, after all, the purpose of the Incarnation. I believe there is a correlation between *expressing love for Jesus* and having the *desire for reconciliation* with Him. When the former is absent, the latter seems unnecessary.

Typically, I write from 5:00 a.m. to 9:00 a.m. For three consecutive days, everything I wrote about reconciliation lacked the force of personal testimony; I was not addressing a compelling question in the mind of the reader. Thursday morning I tried again. I was in our kitchen making coffee and gathering my thoughts. That's when I had my stroke.

I don't know how other people experience strokes. For me, it was a sudden change in vision. The distortion made me feel unbalanced. I walked to the bedroom, sat on the end of the bed, and in response to Pam saying good morning, I announced:

"Something's not right." Twenty minutes later, we were in the emergency room. Still no pain, but it was obvious that something inside had changed. The doctors gave me the entire range of tests — CT scan, MRI, blood work, dexterity test — and diagnosed a mini-stroke. I was fortunate in that my only loss was my field of vision on the left side.

Thursday night, when I was alone in my hospital bed, I prayed. Although this was being called a mini-event, there was the real possibility that another event could happen, especially during the next few days before the medication reached therapeutic effect. I was not afraid of dying, but I explained to Our Lord that this was not the best time. First, there was Pam and our family. It would be so difficult for them. I knew this argument didn't carry much weight, but it was a starting point. Then I reminded Jesus of the assignment He had given me. The new DVD promoting our parish retreats had just been delivered. *We had plans.*

Then I remembered a lighthearted moment during a retreat in Salt Lake City years ago. We were having a discussion on the humanity of Christ, based on a reflection written by Cora Evans, "Jesus, Man of True Cheerfulness." We asked a question for discussion: "What would make Jesus laugh?" One lady took the microphone and said, "You want to make Jesus laugh? Tell Him your plans!" It reminded me that no matter how much I may think God depends on me, God is all-sufficient. If God wants something to happen, it will happen. So right away, my arguments for why Jesus should not take me home at this time melted away.

Later, I read the following unpublished reflection by Cora Evans that validated my thinking:

The chosen few are real captains in My army — they are victims because they are seasoned through study and prayer in the knowledge of the all-sufficient God — God sufficient without them and not needing any help they may offer Him. Thus, in great humility of soul, their torch of light in soul's darkness is the light of trust in the providence of God above their own will.

Cora's reflection humbled me, not that I think of myself as among the chosen few, but the truth that God is all-sufficient. My next prayer was not so self-centered.

I remembered something else Cora Evans had said about prayer. We are never in a better position to pray for someone than when we are suffering. Pray for others who are in the same condition as you but have no one else to pray for them. And so I prayed: "Lord, bless all the stoke victims who feel alone tonight. Bless those with strokes who have no one to pray for them." My train of thought drifted to my good fortune, when compared to the more devastating results of strokes. Here is my dialogue prayer with Jesus:

WOUNDED SOULS

I had a stroke and things aren't right.
My vision is impaired.
Doctors call it a deficit —
such convenient med-speak.
I am wounded,
but there are so many others —
wounded souls who suffer from strokes.

I pray for people who have no one to pray for them.
I pray for those who are alone.
Bless them, Lord.
We are Your wounded souls.
I invite You to relive Your Mystical Humanity,
Your resurrected life,
through me tonight.
I invite You to dwell within my wounded soul,
and together, let us pray for the others.

I was about to fall asleep when there was a knock on the door. "Michael McDevitt? Sorry, I'm dressed in civilian clothes; I was out and just got the call. I'm Father Flavian, a Capuchin Franciscan priest from Our Lady of Angels." After telling me that my ancestors were from the North of Ireland, County Donegal, and that he was from Cork, he asked: "Would you like to receive the Anointing of the Sick?"

It was a question that needed no answer, but my response was an unwavering yes. At that moment, two people who had passed away, Todd and Herb, came to mind.

TODD

Borrowing a relic of Cardinal John Henry Newman from the Newman Club of Los Angeles, I went to pray with my brother-in-law, Todd Kirkpatrick, three months before he died. He was in the final stages of cancer. Todd had been away from the Catholic Church for some time, and I was very apprehensive about praying with him. Before entering his home, I reminded myself that I was not alone. When you talk to someone about faith, the Holy Spirit is always at work in that person. It turned out to be a wonderful, faith-filled experience.

I began by telling Todd about a recent talk I had given to members of the Newman Club and that the club had a relic which was used to pray for the intercession of Cardinal Newman. Then I pulled out the framed relic and told him that Mark Montgomery, the president of the club at the time, had suggested I borrow it for the express purpose of praying with him. Todd's wife, Lynn, was present, and the three of us read the prescribed prayer together. Todd was quite moved and, with tears in his eyes, said: "I'm overwhelmed. . . . I don't know how to thank you."

The prayer opened a door and gave me the courage to take one more step. I suggested that I contact the local parish priest, who could give him the Sacrament of the Anointing of the Sick. Todd appreciated the idea. My next step was to visit the pastor at St. Nicholas Church in Laguna Woods and make the arrangements.

The day I prayed with Todd was just the beginning of his journey home. Sister Mildred Radziewicz, of the Little Company of Mary religious order, director of ministry to the sick at St. Nicholas Parish, visited Todd on several occasions to pray with him. Two days before he died, Todd received his last sacrament, the Anointing of the Sick.

His five adult children gathered from as far away as Alaska and Washington State to be at his bedside in Southern California when he passed away. Later, the parish priest came to their home and held a private Catholic prayer service for Lynn and their children. Although all of the children had been baptized, none of them practiced the faith. It was a powerful experience for them to witness their father's death in the context of faith. They were aware that, in the end, Todd let go and turned to Jesus.

The experience reminded me that God did not come into the world for the saints, but for the people with imperfections. He is looking for the ones who struggle with alcoholism, depression, fear, and complacency. It was remarkable to watch the Holy Spirit work through others to reach Todd, Lynn, and their children.

One month later, one of Todd's daughters called my wife to say that she had decided to go to Christmas Eve Mass, something she had not done for over 20 years. Was there a miracle? I answer with a resounding yes! We prayed for a miracle in the form of physical healing. With God, however, there are spiritual healings — the unseen miracle of salvation.

HERB

Heartened by my experience with Todd, I ventured forward to visit my former college roommate, Herb Sullivan, who was riddled with cancer. A mutual friend and also a former roommate, John Rodee, became the catalyst. John is very active at our alma mater, the University of San Diego. We took Herb to lunch for the purpose of discussing the subject of reconciliation and the Sacrament of the Anointing of the Sick. As a follow-up, John arranged a lunch to introduce Herb to the USD chaplain Father Owen Mullen. Whatever transpired between Herb and Father Owen is personal, between them and Our Lord.

It was less than a year later, while driving to a retreat, that I received word that Herb had suffered a massive stroke. He passed away the next day. For me, it was a harsh reality to recall that Herb had not had the same opportunity to receive the Anointing of the Sick that I had been given. His stroke completely disabled him and rendered him unconscious. But I was comforted by the realization that near the end of his life, Herb connected with a Catholic priest. He approached death with an open heart — the kind of heart that is infused with the mercy of God.

MY EXPERIENCE

Over the years, I have witnessed other people receiving the sacrament, and there is an undeniable feeling of satisfaction. This time I was in the hospital. Never before had I been in a situation like this — thinking about my own mortality, praying and coping. I listened to Father Flavian as he prayed the formula for absolution:

> God, Father of mercies,
> through the death and the resurrection of his Son
> has reconciled the world to himself
> and sent the Holy Spirit among us
> for the forgiveness of sins;
> through the ministry of the Church
> may God give you pardon and peace,
> and I absolve you from your sins
> in the name of the Father, and of the Son,
> and of the Holy Spirit.

After giving me the Apostolic Pardon, Father Flavian added: "You have received a plenary indulgence, and all the sins of your whole life are forgiven."

I was overwhelmed. Father anointed me on the forehead and hands with blessed oil and continued the prayer:

Through this holy anointing
may the Lord in his love and mercy help you
with the grace of the Holy Spirit....
May the Lord, who frees you from sin,
save you and raise you up.

After the concluding blessing, he left. Alone in the darkness of my hospital room, I realized that I had received the "last sacrament" — preparation for the final journey to eternal life. My prayers changed. God had granted me pardon, and now I felt amazing peace.

In those quiet moments, I understood St. Paul's teaching about God reconciling the world to Himself "in Christ" (see 2 Cor 5:19). An accurate paraphrase is "by means of Jesus." I knew that I possessed Him and was possessed by Him. The reality of this oneness with Jesus Christ brought me closer to every one of God's children. Gratitude was the only prayer I could express. I was in the eternal life-giving presence of Jesus, and all I had to offer in return for this magnificent gift — salvation — were a few words of appreciation. It was fitting that I closed my eyes and fell asleep.

Because of my experience, I now have something to say about reconciliation: If you do not have the desire for reconciliation, something is missing. Pray about it. Do not wait until the end of your life to be reconciled with God. Express your love for Jesus without hesitation. Take Jesus with you each day so that when you reach the end of this earthly life, He is right there, a familiar friend, welcoming you home. Imagine Jesus with His arms outstretched. He is like the little boy playing hide-and-seek. He is overjoyed to allow you to see Him for the first time. He can hardly wait.

CHAPTER FOUR

Pray the Mass

"The most meaningful part for me was the 'real presence in the Eucharist.' The Mass was the highlight. The liturgy and the blessing were truly the work of the Spirit and inspired me. I will focus on the Eucharist more and trust God to do His will in my life. It keeps our hearts open to live our life as God has planned for us, and to use our gifts to serve Him and our brothers and sisters daily."

RETREAT PARTICIPANT

To appreciate the Mass, we must first be aware of the earliest form of prayer, especially that of the Jews, leading up to the Last Supper.

In the Old Testament, we learn the purpose of ancient prayers: worship and praise, petition, gratitude, and reconciliation. Prayer took the form of offering a sacrifice to God. Our first example is Cain and Abel, the children of Adam and Eve, who worshiped God in the form of offering gifts: fruits and vegetables, and an animal. Their offerings were placed on kindling and destroyed by fire, hence the name "burnt offerings." By having their offerings destroyed, they were giving the best of what they owned and offering it completely to God. By offering an animal as his sacrifice, Abel was parting with something of far greater value than the harvest offered by his brother. The sense of parting with something of value was at the heart of prayer. This form of prayer, offering a sacrifice to God as the way of illustrating personal surrender, continued right up to and immediately following the time of Christ.

When Noah exited the ark, he built an altar of stone and offered a sacrifice as an expression of gratitude. Abraham was willing to offer his only son as a sacrifice to demonstrate his complete surrender to God's will. There are numerous examples of offering something back to God as the primary form of prayer, but it is the story of Moses that helps us connect the dots between the customs of old and our Mass today.

THE LAMB OF MOSES

When Pharaoh refused to listen to the admonitions of God, Moses said to all the people: "Select lambs for yourselves according to your families, and kill the Passover lamb" (Ex 12:21).

Moses and Aaron instructed the Israelites to select a yearling lamb without blemish to be sacrificed to God. Every family was directed to sprinkle their doorpost with the blood of their lamb and consume it as the meal, along with unleavened bread (baked without yeast) and bitter herbs (wild lettuce). They did as they were commanded, and then "at midnight the LORD struck all the first-born in the land of Egypt, from the first-born of Pharaoh who sat on his throne to the first-born of the captive who was in the dungeon, and all the first-born of the cattle" (Ex 12:29). But God did not strike the houses of the Jews because they were sprinkled with the blood of the lamb. That same night Pharaoh ordered the Israelites to leave Egypt immediately, thus beginning the Exodus and the passage through the Red Sea.

The Lord instructed Moses and Aaron:

> "This day shall be for you a memorial day, and you shall keep it as a feast to the LORD; throughout your generations you shall observe it as an ordinance for ever. . . . And when your children say to you, 'What do you mean by this service?' you shall say, 'It is the sacrifice of the Lord's Passover, for he passed over the houses of the sons of Israel in Egypt, when he slew the Egyptians but spared our houses.'" And the people bowed their heads and worshiped. (Ex 12:14, 26-27)

Today, Jews observe Passover as the feast to commemorate the exodus to freedom that began when the Lord passed over the houses of the Israelites. Lamb is served to memorialize the great event.

THE LAMB OF GOD

At the Last Supper, Jesus instituted the Eucharist. Henceforth, the Mass would be the only perfect form of worship. The sacrifice of Jesus is perfect: no mere lamb, He is the all-perfect Lamb of God. Jesus offered Himself as the new Lamb to be sacrificed on the altar. He said it would not be necessary to offer a lamb at all — "*Do this* in memory of me!" (see Lk 22:19 and 1 Cor 11:24-25). With the offering of Himself, Jesus abolished the ancient forms of sacrifice and created the New

Covenant, which offers redemption, forgiveness, and salvation. No person or event compares to the magnitude of this direct connection that God, the Creator of all that is, offered to everyone in the world.

Today, the Catholic priest, by virtue of the Sacrament of Holy Orders, acts in the person of Christ because the presence of Christ is permanent — dwelling within him at all times. This is the eternal mark of the ministerial priesthood. The Sacrament of Holy Orders confers a unique gift of the Holy Spirit that permits the exercise of a sacred power: the incomparable privilege of offering the Mass, the event in which the original redemptive sacrifice of Christ (the Last Supper, His Passion and death, and His resurrection) is made present.

HOW TO PRAY THE MASS

To fully appreciate the Mass, it is helpful to imagine the events of the Last Supper. Imagine the twelve apostles reclining around a horseshoe-shaped table, with Jesus in the middle of them. Imagine the dress, the customs of the day, the reclining pillows, the wooden bowls, and the friendly conversations. There is a sense of excitement and anticipation in the room. Imagine the meal of lamb, with Jesus as the host, passing around pieces of lamb wrapped in wild lettuce leaves just like the first Passover feast. As the meal ends, imagine the apostles wondering among themselves if this would be the occasion for Jesus, their Lord, to give them the living bread as He had promised.

Scripture does not tell us if Mary was present. The custom of the day would place her there with other women, who would prepare and serve the meal, so it is likely that the Blessed

Mother was there. Imagine her bringing forward the chalice and the bread. Imagine the stillness, the quiet that overtakes the room as Jesus begins the blessing of the bread and wine. Peter must have been overwhelmed. How did Peter respond when Jesus handed him the first Eucharist — the living bread, the new everlasting Lamb of God? No longer would there be the need to celebrate the Exodus symbolized in the Jewish Passover meal. Imagine how you might respond if you were present.

INTRODUCTORY AND PENITENTIAL RITES

When you attend Mass, do not think of yourself as part of an audience attending a play. This is more than replicating the words of Jesus at the Last Supper. The invisible miracle is about to take place.

Our community prayer begins when the priest greets the faithful: "The grace of our Lord Jesus Christ and the love of God / and the fellowship of the Holy Spirit be with you all." As a community we respond, "And also with you."

Here is one of the prayers the priest says as we call to mind our sins: "As we prepare to celebrate the mystery of Christ's love, / let us acknowledge our failures / and ask the Lord for pardon and strength." Again, as one community we respond, "I confess to almighty God, / and to you, my brothers and sisters, / that I have sinned through my own fault / in my thoughts and in my words, / in what I have done, / and in what I have failed to do. . . ."

From the very beginning, you are making yourself ready to receive Jesus. You are a temple, and Jesus is about to enter. This is the time to prepare your temple.

LITURGY OF THE WORD

Liturgy, the ritual public worship of the faithful, has always made use of Sacred Scripture. When we refer to Scripture as sacred — meaning divinely inspired — we rely on the belief of the apostles and the doctrine of our faith:

> For holy mother Church, relying on the belief of the Apostles (see John 20:31; 2 Tim. 3:16; 2 Peter 1:19-20, 3:15-16), holds that the books of both the Old and New Testaments in their entirety, with all their parts, are sacred and canonical because written under the inspiration of the Holy Spirit, *they have God as their author* and have been handed on as such to the Church herself. . . . [I]n the sacred books, the Father who is in heaven meets His children with great love and speaks with them. (Second Vatican Council, *Dei Verbum*, Dogmatic Constitution on Divine Revelation [November 18, 1965], nn. 11, 21; emphasis added)

The next time you hear the Scripture readings and the concluding statements "The word of the Lord" and "The gospel of the Lord," recall that God is the author. With this awareness, your responses "Thanks be to God" and "Praise to you, Lord Jesus Christ" will have the meaning for which they are intended. Tradition teaches us that the Holy Spirit is at work in human hearts and brings all people of faith to an understanding of what God has revealed. Receive the Word with reverence.

The First Reading, from the Old Testament, is in preparation for the coming of Jesus. The Second Reading and the Gospel reading, from the New Testament, are about Jesus and

His message for us. Once again, we are being called to follow Him. Listen to the Word for inspiration. For example, rather than thinking of St. Paul as writing just to his community, recognize that Our Lord inspired Paul. When you hear Paul's words, it is the Lord Himself trying to reach you personally. The same is true for all of Scripture.

In the homily, God's word is spoken through the priest, who attempts to make the message of Scripture relevant to you. There is a vast range in the effectiveness of homilies. As a participant in the Mass, you have a role to play in the readings and the homily: the willingness and desire to listen and learn. There is meaning for you, and it is your responsibility to discover it. At every Mass, Jesus is offering you an opportunity to gain insight into the mystery of faith. For you, there will be no disconnect unless you allow it. Ask Jesus to help you understand Scripture. Prepare yourself to receive Him into your humble heart as you recite the creed: ". . . and for our salvation / he came down from heaven." He is about to come down from heaven again, and you are going to greet Him in person.

The first part of our two-part liturgy prepares us to enter into the Eucharistic sacrifice. Scripture is always new, always instructive, if we deem it an opportunity to gain knowledge. Gradually, we remove ourselves from the clutter and demands of everyday life. We make ourselves approachable so as to draw near the One Who is coming. The priest will make present the events of 2,000 years ago.

LITURGY OF THE EUCHARIST

To pray the Mass is to engage. To engage, you must be open to the insights Our Lord wants to share with you. By approaching the table of the Lord with an open heart, you are allowing the work of the Holy Spirit to be accomplished. Unlike reading a book with footnotes and facts that are easy to comprehend, the mystery of God is revealed through fractions of insight, a gradual process that draws you closer to Him.

There is so much to be gained by attending Mass that it defies description. It is not a deed that shows God you are in attendance as required by the doctrine of the Catholic Church. Such an approach to Mass is an injustice and a dishonest response to what you know to be true. Our Lord has invited you to do more than go through the motions. He is about to give Himself to you — to you *personally.*

Prepare to bow before the kingship of Christ. Pray for wisdom. Pray that on this day you will come just a bit closer to understanding His mission in the world and the role He wants you to play in it. Pray that by receiving Him in the Eucharist, you will be renewed in your faith. Pray to understand the meaning of St. Paul's statement: "Therefore, if any one is in Christ, he is a new creation; the old has passed away, behold, the new has come" (2 Cor 5:17). Pray for the insight to share in the faith, hope, and love of all the faithful. This could be the last Mass you ever attend. Pray that it lasts forever.

THE TABLE OF THE LORD

The altar is prepared; the gifts of bread and wine for the celebration are brought up by members of the congregation. The prayer of the priest standing at the altar initiates the Liturgy of the Eucharist:

Blessed are you, Lord, God of all creation.
Through your goodness we have this bread to offer,
which earth has given and human hands have made.
It will become for us the bread of life.

You've heard it a hundred times. Pray about the last sentence — this ordinary bread will be consecrated and become the bread of eternal life. The miracle is unfolding: "By the mystery of this water and wine / may we come to share in the divinity of Christ, / who humbled himself to share in our humanity."

The whole congregation joins in asking that Jesus accept our offering. The Prayer Over the Gifts changes from one week to the next. Here is one example (26th Sunday in Ordinary Time, Year C): "God of mercy, / accept our offering / and make it a source of blessing for us. / We ask this in the name of Jesus the Lord."

With these common prayers, we are opening our hearts to God in humility. The priest says, "Lift up your hearts," and we respond, "We lift them up to the Lord." For you personally, this is like saying, "I am opening my heart to You, Jesus."

LISTEN TO JESUS

The Eucharistic Prayer states the central theme of the Mass, "We come to you, Father, / with praise and thanksgiving, / through Jesus Christ your Son."* We pray for our pope and bishops, and for all the faithful, especially those who are gathered on this occasion. We honor Mary, Joseph, and the apostles

---

* There are four Eucharistic Prayers. This text is taken from Eucharistic Prayer I.

and martyrs. Then the priest calls us to remember the Lord's Supper:

> He broke the bread,
> gave it to his disciples and said [and now the priest, with Christ dwelling within him, speaks in the first person, in the person of Christ Himself]: Take this, all of you, and eat it:
> this is my body which will be given up for you.

Again, with the chalice raised, Christ speaks to you just as He spoke to His apostles 2,000 years ago:

> [T]his is the cup of my blood,
> the blood of the new and everlasting covenant.

It is Jesus Who presides invisibly over every Eucharistic celebration. You recognize the voice of the priest, but it is the resurrected Christ speaking through him. Respond in your heart — not to the sound of the voice, but to the speaker, Jesus Christ (see *Catechism of the Catholic Church*, n. 1348).

EMBRACE THE MYSTERY OF FAITH

When Jesus spoke these words for the first time, He was instituting the Eucharist — the one single sacrifice of Himself, "for you and for all / so that sins may be forgiven." The Mass does not repeat what happened at the Lord's Supper; rather, it connects you with it. The host you receive, Holy Communion, is the same "bread of life" received by Peter and the apostles, by the saints down through the centuries, and by all those who have gone before us and all who will come after. There is one God, one Eucharist. There is a single sacrifice of Jesus on the cross. Pray to understand and embrace this celebrated mystery of faith. There is nothing else, no other form of prayer, like this intimate connection between God and you.

OFFER YOURSELF

You involve yourself in the Mass by offering yourself to God. Bring it all to the table: suffering, heartbreak, disappointment, joy, gratitude, and the exciting good news in your life. This is the essence of what you have to offer. Listen to the words of St. Paul: "I appeal to you therefore, brethren, by the mercies of God, to present your bodies as a living sacrifice, holy and acceptable to God, which is your spiritual worship" (Rom 12:1-2). By uniting yourself as an offering at Mass, you fully participate in what is taking place — "Through him, with him, in him."

You present yourself as a gift to God through a prayer that states your intentions: "Lord, I offer myself to You." Just as Jesus gives all of Himself to us by His presence in the Eucharist — His joy; His suffering, sacrifice, and sorrow; His death and His resurrection — so you have an opportunity to give all of yourself back to Him. It is the finest gift you have to offer. Here is a prayer for the occasion:

Take me, Lord. I bring it all to You: my life with the suffering and pain; my life with the grief and sorrow I am experiencing; the sacrifices I must make for the sake of others; and the loneliness I encounter. Take me, Lord. I give my life to You, with all its joy and happiness. Lord,

I surrender it all to You. I offer it as my humble gift. I pray that You will incorporate my heart into Your Sacred Heart. I give You all that I am and all that I have. I come to You in gratitude and pray that You will accept this offering.

With this prayer, or your own version of it, you become a courageous witness to faith. You know, and Jesus appreciates, the spiritual value of your circumstances in life. You unite yourself completely with Our Lord, and He accepts your gift of self just as He accepts you, embraces you, and loves you.

THE PERFECT PRAYER

Surrender yourself; empty yourself of self to make room for Jesus. Surrender yourself so that the hidden power of God can live within you and act through you. Present yourself as an offering, and unite your offering to that of Christ's. Pray the Mass, and your soul will radiate His divine life; your daily life will become the means of worshiping God with undivided love.

During Mass, we recite the mystery of faith: "Christ has died, / Christ is risen, / Christ will come again." You live in the gap between "Christ is risen" and "Christ will come again." The work of the Incarnation is not completed. Jesus has risen, and there is a profound mission to be accomplished before He comes again. That is why the Eucharist is essential. With it, you take Him into the world to bring about His works of mercy and love.

At Mass (Eucharistic Prayer III), we pray: "Grant that we, who are nourished by his body and blood, / may be filled with

his Holy Spirit, / and become one body, one spirit in Christ."
Then we say a thought-provoking intercessory prayer: "May
he [Jesus] make us an everlasting gift to you. . . ." You are asking Jesus to make you a gift to the Father. This is your perfect
prayer because Jesus accepts your offer and unites you to Himself as a gift to the Father. When you receive the Eucharist,
your offering is complete.

THE MAGNITUDE OF HIS LOVE

Father Frank said this to retreatants gathered at Colombiere
House, his residence in Southern California:

> He [Jesus] loves each one of you so much that he would
> have died for you alone. He would have climbed up the
> cross of Calvary and died for you, and He dies in the
> mystical, unbloody manner in the Mass that we might
> continue His life through our humanities. We become
> His Mystical Humanity.

Imagine the magnitude of God's love for each one of us.
He then continued:

> This is exactly what our dear Lord wants us to do — to
> spread His divine life and human life dwelling within us.
> Not only does Jesus give us His own divine life, but He
> gives us His human life as well. Haven't we always said,
> since children, the Eucharist is the Body and Blood, Soul
> and Divinity of Jesus? And I believe this, and I believed
> it all my life, and I believe that is probably the reason
> why I became a Jesuit priest. This is the spirituality of

St. Ignatius: the humanity of Jesus dwells within us — as well as the divinity. We are taking Christ's place in the world of today, which is so engulfed in materialism and things of time and pleasure, of here and now, that people are not aware or don't leave themselves open to be aware of the divine gift of God dwelling within them.

THE ONE BODY OF CHRIST

The personal connection you have with Jesus is enjoyed by all members of Christ's faithful. The Eucharist creates this unity in the most perfect way, because through your participation you become one with Jesus in the same way that all of His faithful become one with Him. We are reminded of this truth when the priest says the final prayer of praise, "Through him, / with him, / in him, / in the unity of the Holy Spirit, / all glory and honor is yours, / almighty Father, / for ever and ever." The spiritual connection that unites us extends from the time of Christ until the end of time. This is the manner in which we are part of the Mystical Body of Christ, and why we can never be closer to one another — and to those who have passed away — than when we receive the Eucharist.

THE MEANING OF PARTICIPATION

To paraphrase Pope Benedict XVI: The words of the priest at Mass are not sufficient; it took Jesus' death on the cross to make it a real sacrifice. The words of the priest and the cross are insufficient; it took the Resurrection to give the Sacrifice of the Mass its divine authority. All three — the words, the cross, and the Resurrection — are still insufficient; it takes your participation to give the Lord's Supper its meaning.

Participation is more than showing up. It is about praying the Mass by offering yourself to God and welcoming Him into your heart and soul.

ABRAHAM

Our Lord instructed Abraham to take Isaac to Mount Moria to sacrifice his son as a holocaust (a sacrifice in which the victim — an animal — was first killed, and then wholly burnt). Without hesitation, although he must have wondered why God would ask such a thing of him, Abraham took several servants and Isaac and left on the sorrowful journey. After several days, Abraham and Isaac left company of the servants and made the final climb. There is a wonderful line in Scripture which captures the image of Abraham: "And he took in his hand the fire [hot coals in a vessel] and the knife" (Gen 22:6).

In this story, Abraham is more than a hundred years old. He is a man of strength and courage. He is a man willing to do anything to prove his love for God. The story concludes with last-minute intervention by an angel. Although Abraham is willing to sacrifice his son, Isaac is saved. They find a ram (male sheep) in the bushes, and this animal becomes their offering. Then the angel delivers God's promise to multiply Abraham's seed, and from his seed the Savior would be born.

Today, you are like Abraham, carrying fire and a sword. The sword is your willingness to defend the faith. Unlike Abraham, the fire you carry is not a vessel with hot coals; it is the indwelling of Christ. You have become alive with the life of Christ, and you take Him with you wherever you go.

~~

CHAPTER FIVE

Pray With Mary and Joseph

"When we stand before an extraordinary minister of the Eucharist and receive the Eucharist, we are like Mary, saying yes to God. We accept being the tabernacle for His flesh and blood, and bond to Him by the umbilical cord of faith."

RETREAT PARTICIPANT

"I love the image of Joseph carrying the infant Jesus. He appears to be presenting Jesus with such delight. I should have the same fulfillment after I receive the Jesus in the Eucharist. Joseph was the guardian of the Redeemer 2,000 years ago. I'm His guardian today."

RETREAT PARTICIPANT

For years, I struggled to appreciate my relationship with the Blessed Mother. My focus had been on Jesus, almost to the exclusion of His mother. When people would share their stories of meeting the visionaries in Medjugorje, I would shrug my shoulders. It wasn't that I did not believe them, but someone else's experience didn't do anything for my faith. I had a problem. Why was I not closer to the Mother of Jesus? So I prayed about it: "Jesus, help me to understand what You want for Your mother. Mary, help me to understand what you want for your Son."

The answer to my prayer came in an unexpected way. My partner, Rob Bussell, and I had just finished facilitating a one-day retreat for St. Ambrose Parish in Salt Lake City. During our debriefing session with Pam Avery, director of religious education, she asked if we could do a retreat that featured the new Luminous Mysteries of the Rosary. Over the years, we developed the capability of customizing retreats to tie in with a number of themes: the Sacred Heart, unity, the Indwelling, and the Eucharist, to name a few. We had not yet highlighted the Rosary, but we knew we could deliver. Jesus was about to tell me what He wants for His mother.

When Pope John Paul II's new mysteries — the Mysteries of Light, or the Luminous Mysteries — were announced, I was curious. I read the Pope's apostolic letter on the Rosary, *Rosarium Virginis Mariae*, and for the first time realized that I had misunderstood the Rosary — I knew how to *say* it, but not how to *pray* it. My version of saying the Rosary was mere words, not the contemplation of the life of Jesus. I understood the mechanics of the Rosary, but not how to use it as a form of meditation. Unfortunately for me, I was not deriving the spiritual benefits the Rosary had to offer. When I did say it, I might plow through it while listening to the car radio. Another way was to visualize a person in my family and offer a Hail Mary for my wife, my daughters, my son, my grandchildren, then my brothers and sister, and so forth. While it is good to pray for members of my family, the Rosary is designed to be a means of meditating on the life of Jesus. That is its purpose and value.

THE EXQUISITE PRAYER

The first step in praying the Rosary is to visualize Mary with Jesus, beginning with His infancy and childhood, through adolescence, young adulthood, and finally manhood. She raised Jesus, she knew who He was, and she understood her motherly role. She listened to His words, watched Him relate to others, and witnessed many of the events we read about in Scripture. She experienced much more than we know in the bond that exists between a mother and her son. Jesus treated her with all the respect motherhood demands. He was proud of her, proud to introduce her to His friends, and we can imagine Him saying, "This is my mother." To Mary, Jesus would always be "my son." The memories of her Son's life are forever etched in her heart (see Lk 2:19). It is her memories we tap into when we *pray* the Rosary.

In his apostolic letter, Pope John Paul II states: "In the recitation of the Rosary, the Christian community enters into contact with the memories and the contemplative gaze of Mary." Allow me to personalize his statement: "When I pray the Rosary, I enter into contact with the memories of Mary, the memories she has about the life of Jesus." The Holy Father then reminds us of the contemplative nature of the Rosary: "Precisely because it starts with Mary's own experience, [the Rosary] is *an exquisitely contemplative prayer*. Without this contemplative dimension, it would lose its meaning" (*Rosarium Virginis Mariae*, On the Most Holy Rosary [October 16, 2002], nn. 11, 12; emphasis in the original).

So the Rosary is a form of prayer that contemplates the life of Jesus in union with Mary. The scenes in the life of Jesus are joyful, sorrowful, and glorious, and they also center on His public ministry in the Luminous Mysteries. We call them "mysteries" because they remind us of the earthly life of the Son of God, and the Incarnation is the unfathomable mystery of God.

"The Eucharistic faith of Mary showed its first fruits most powerfully when, in humility and pure love, she said yes at the Annunciation. As the 'Eternal Yes,' she always joyfully and trustingly did, and continues to do, the will of God. Nothing pleases her more. She wants the souls of all humanity to come to her Son."

RETREAT PARTICIPANT

THE EVERLASTING AFFIRMATION

During the process of getting reacquainted with Mary, I thought about how she might answer my reoccurring question: "What does a mother want for her son?" I thought about the unique role of Mary. In all of history, there never has been another person like her, nor will there be again. Just as I accept the real presence of Jesus in the Eucharist as a matter of faith, I also accept that Mary was conceived without the taint of Adam and Eve's original sin. We call this the Immaculate Conception, and it is dogma of the Catholic faith.*

From the very beginning of her life, Mary was spiritually set apart. Her spotless soul is like that of Adam and Eve before

---

* The dogma of the Immaculate Conception was declared by Pope Pius IX, in his apostolic constitution *Ineffabilis Deus* ("God Ineffable"), December 8, 1854. Dogma is a definitive teaching of the Catholic Church and is considered part of divine revelation. The Church expresses dogma in a solemn decree or as a universal teaching. As such, a formal and deliberate rejection of a dogma is an act of heresy. For more information, see the *Catechism of the Catholic Church*, nn. 88-90 and 2089.

their fall, and she is therefore a new creation. She remained faithful to her unique calling throughout her life and was thus prepared to respond to the extraordinary appearance of the angel Gabriel.

These are powerful reflections. As I stirred these thoughts about Mary in my mind, I developed a sense of appreciation for her. The experience has been like getting to know an acquaintance better and better. Gradually, our relationship matured into a friendship. I became especially appreciative of the free choice she made when the angel Gabriel appeared to her: "Behold, I am the handmaid of the Lord; let it be to me according to your word" (Lk 1:38). Mary's "yes" was the affirmation that would last forever. It was more than a positive response to a question; it was a commitment that would forever change her life, and ours. Hidden in our reflections about Mary is the fact that she had a free will and a choice to say, "Could you come back later? I'm busy right now." At that moment she could have rejected God. But she said yes.

SHE CAPTURED MY HEART

The connection between Mary and the Eucharist is illuminating. I appreciate the humanity of Mary, her role during the life of Jesus, and I have gained a new understanding of her role as it relates to me today. What does Jesus want for His mother, as it relates to my life? He wants me to accept her, just as I accept my own mother. And what does Mary, the Blessed Mother, want for her Son, as it relates to my life? Mary wants me to invite her Son to dwell within me, to live His Mystical Humanity through me. Only in this way can her Son's work, the work for which she nourished Him throughout His life, continue. I know that she will do everything in her power to unite us all in this magnificent endeavor. As we encounter the conflicts of daily life, she is there to encourage us in ways reserved for mothers.

The retreat featuring the Rosary was held at St. Ambrose Parish as promised. The theme was "A Day With Jesus and Mary: Celebrating the New Mysteries of Light." Our retreats combine faith-sharing with lectures. Mass is always the center-piece. In fact, we will not do a retreat without the Eucharist. The homily theme on this day was about Mary, the first tab-ernacle in history. It was especially insightful.

The experience at St. Ambrose was wonderful. We pro-vided readings and discussion questions for each of the five mysteries:

- *The Baptism of Jesus* (see Mt 3:13-17): With our bap-tism, we become stakeholders in the mission of Christ. In what way do you participate in His mission?
- *The Wedding at Cana* (see Jn 2:1-11): What was the communication between Mary and Jesus that made Him perform the sign of changing water into wine?
- *The Proclamation of the Kingdom* (see Mk 1:14-15): How can you courageously identify and denounce evil?
- *The Transfiguration* (see Lk 9:28-36): Why do you think that Peter, James, and John did not speak of what they had seen?
- *The Institution of the Eucharist* (see Mt 26:26-29): How does the Eucharist sustain you?

In the afternoon, following our discussions and participa-tion in Mass, there was a strong sense of unity among the whole group. We listened to a recording of the Rosary, which included inspirational music, and reflected on each mystery in silence. In the process, Mary answered my prayer. I know what she wants for her Son. And she captured my heart.

She is the Blessed Mother; she is my mother.

JOSEPH

When Scripture describes St. Joseph as "a just man" (Mt 1:19), we view him as a young man with a reputation that set him apart from the crowd. We know he was held in high esteem, respected for his honesty and appreciated for his sincerity.

While the "just" designation gives us some insight into his character, the term falls short of telling us about the man in terms of his emotions. We know the decisions he made, and we can track his movements. We know something of his work ethic and his field of interest; he was a carpenter and, as envisioned by Cora Evans, a mapmaker.

But to get to know the person, we rely on our imagination and our own life experiences. We understand how Joseph felt, to the degree that we once felt that way, too. We understand how Joseph lived out his faith because we are attempting to do the same thing. It is precisely because we do not have all the details of his life, and are left to fill in the blanks, that Joseph becomes the ideal model for contemplative and imagination prayer.

IMAGINATION PRAYER

In our solitude, we imagine the life of St. Joseph. Thanks to movies and artist renderings, it is easy to imagine the young man, his physical appearance, the community, the dwellings, the marketplace, his personal living quarters, a gathering of friends, and the surrounding environment. In your imagination, visualize Joseph in a setting that took place 2,000 years ago.

My devotion to St. Joseph is relatively new. It was not a "target" on my spiritual radar until an unusual series of events seemed to unfold around me. Now Joseph stands above all other saints as my go-to person in meditative prayer.

It began with the decision Pam and I made to sign up for a three-day silent retreat to be given by our spiritual guide, Father Vito Perrone.

The next piece of the puzzle was supplied a few weeks later by my cousin, Mary Jean DuPont. As I was leaving her home in Southern California after a short stay, she handed me a piece of paper with a novena to St. Joseph, saying, "I thought you might find this interesting."

The final piece of the puzzle was added by Father Vito when he asked me to give a talk on the retreat and said, "We are using St. Joseph as a model for contemplative prayer." The novena became the centerpiece of my talk, and I recommended St. Joseph as the perfect model for contemplation on a silent retreat. The following is an example.

CONTEMPLATION WITH JOSEPH

Throughout the process of contemplation, you imagine the setting and identify with the emotion of this incomparable saint. It is a small leap of imagination. There is a holiness that blankets the reflection. This is an ordinary man who is suddenly thrust into a heretofore unknown situation. No person has ever been offered such a role. It is preordained by God, but at first Joseph does not know that. And so your reflection begins with Joseph and his willingness to cooperate with grace.

Before he knows the full story, Joseph must feel anguish when he discovers that Mary is with child. How can this be? It is devastating news. His first reaction is disbelief. That reaction gives way to anger. Finally, he is reconciled to the reality of what he thinks is true and resolves to divorce her quietly so that no harm or embarrassment will come to her. It is only after this turmoil and considerable anxiety and confusion that the angel appears to him:

> "Joseph, son of David, do not fear to take Mary your wife, for that which is conceived in her is of the Holy Spirit." (Mt 1:20)

He never doubts the message he has received from the angel. He asks for clarification, and then, without hesitation, says yes!

As you stir these thoughts in your imagination, thank God for the graces Joseph received, and ask through the intercession of St. Joseph that you have the courage to cooperate with the graces God gives to you.

THE ENCOUNTER

What was it like when Joseph and Mary reunited; their first encounter after Joseph did as the angel of the Lord commanded? I get spiritual pleasure from imagining a reunion where no words are spoken. Mary sees Joseph and can tell by the look on his face that all is well. He knows the truth. Rather than jump for joy they stand close, holding each other's hands while facing one another and making eye contact. I freeze-frame the moment in my thoughts. Words are not necessary as the couple absorbs the gravity of their graces. This is one of the most profound moments in all of history. Now they are a family — the Holy Family.

Mary and Joseph do not know how their future will unfold. This is God's plan, they think, and they will cooperate with every grace and face every challenge together. It is easy to become engrossed in this image. I like to stay in this moment of prayer and linger for a while to let the magnitude of their example sink in.

Isn't it true that all of us face an uncertain future? For a married couple, the example of Mary and Joseph is one of commitment. They do not know where Jesus will be born. They do not know that King Herod will order their child to be captured and killed. They do not know the ending of the story. What they do know is that God is with them, and that they have each other.

Before continuing to the next segment of Joseph's life, ask God, through the intercession of St. Joseph, to guide you in your special relationships, as you pray for your spouse, each member of your family, and all your loved ones.

JOSEPH'S WAY OF PRAYER

As your contemplation of St. Joseph evolves, imagine his personal prayer life. Imagine Joseph in a sacred space, in solitude, in his personal place for daily prayer. He does not have a prayer book to guide him — only his thoughts and recollections of Scripture stories. I also like to visualize the saint taking a walk near his home in the early evening hours.

At times, Joseph must have thought: "Why did you choose me, Lord? I am just a simple soul." At another time, I can visualize Joseph reciting psalms from memory: "I will give thanks to the LORD with my whole heart; / I will tell of all your wonderful deeds. / I will be glad and exult in you; / I will sing praise to your name, O Most High" (Ps 9:1-2). Perhaps he recalled, "Awesome is God in his sanctuary, / the God of Israel, / he gives power and strength to his people. / Blessed be God!" (Ps 68:35).

There were many secrets in Joseph's life that he could not share with others. He must have visited with God in frequent dialogue prayer. What do you think the spirituality of Joseph was like? And how do you think he shared his experience of faith with Mary? Conclude your reflections by asking for God's guidance, through the intercession of St. Joseph, in the ways of quiet prayer, as you enter the silence of solitude.

JOSEPH EXPRESSES HIS LOVE

When I contemplate Joseph and his attitude toward Mary, I visualize him as having a depth of love that is willing to do literally anything to please her. While he recognizes his role as guardian of the Redeemer, she is the Mother of God! Every day, in his own way, he says: "I love you, Mary." I think of Joseph as a gentle man who liked to find creative ways of expressing his feelings, small things like carving a small wooden vase and filling it with wildflowers as a simple gesture of letting her know how special she is in his eyes. And so the meditation goes.

Allow your mind to wander, and imagine what this most beautiful of relationships might have been like. Then thank

God for the love of Joseph for Mary and pray, through the intercession of St. Joseph, that you develop the same love for the Mother of God.

JOSEPH'S RELATIONSHIP WITH JESUS

St. Joseph was the leader, the guardian, and the worker who provided for his family. To Jesus, he was a loving father and a teacher. I imagine Joseph taking Jesus on a walk and having a father-son conversation. I wonder what he might have said. I wonder how he manifested his love for Jesus. I wonder what lessons he taught. And I wonder how Joseph responded to the wisdom of his Son.

As a five-year-old child, Jesus had playthings. Joseph likely got down on the ground and joined in the make-believe games. Maybe they had a foot race, played catch, and cared for a pet animal together. I can visualize Jesus sitting on the workbench, watching and listening as Joseph plied his trade.

Isn't it fascinating that without having any of the details about the daily life of the Holy Family, we can contemplate how they responded to grace, prayed together, expressed their love for one another, conducted their own prayer in solitude, and engaged in dialogue prayer?

CHAPTER SIX

Engage in Dialogue Prayer

"This retreat experience brought me closer to Jesus at a time in my life when I most needed Him — when I was diagnosed with breast cancer. While receiving chemotherapy, I attended one of your parish retreats. It was the year 2000. After that retreat, I invited Jesus to walk every step with me. He never left me. He blessed me with an inner peace, which I cannot describe. God bless you in this ministry."

RETREAT PARTICIPANT

Jesus will draw all people to Himself (see Jn 12:32). Therefore, it is to Jesus that we pray. It is with Jesus that we connect in a dialogue of love. You were created to love God — to praise, glorify, and serve God, and in the process to achieve your eternal destiny. The spirituality taught here positions faith as a continuous dialogue between you and Jesus. This spirituality helps you understand Who it is that you are praising, glorifying, and serving. This is especially helpful in a world in which you are constantly confronted with ambiguity and change. You engage in a dialogue with Jesus that is unambiguous. Your continuous dialogue teaches you Who Jesus is and how to understand your relationship with Him.

ON WRITING PRAYERS

One energizing next step is to commit your dialogue prayer to written prayer. I urge you to begin writing prayers. It is a form of giving praise to God in a beautiful, personal way. The activity of writing is in itself a form of prayer. A good starting point is to keep a spiritual journal, a place where you record your inspirational thoughts and blessed ideas.

There is nothing special about my prayers; they are shared here as an example of writing to pray. They capture my thoughts about our fast-paced environment, family life, teenagers, and children in general. One prayer may be a reflection on the suffering of Christ; another may focus on unity and the reality that we are all in this together. There are prayers about the Bread of life, the Incarnation and our participation in it, and the Risen Christ.

"Alive With the Life of Christ" is an example of writing a prayer that speaks to the meaning of living, with the uplifting thought that the Spirit of God is dwelling in us. It is the ultimate affirmation of what we Christians know by faith to be true. It propels our faith forward, from acknowledging beliefs to a new level of awareness of this truth daily — even hourly.

This does not mean that you walk around with your hands together as though in prayer, nor does it separate you from others. Quite the opposite is the true-life experience. You realize how much you have in common with other people, regardless of culture, income, or lifestyle. When you are alive with Christ, the barriers come down. Your connection with Him is your connection with everyone else. With this mindset, I wrote this dialogue prayer:

ALIVE WITH THE LIFE OF CHRIST

I am alive with the indwelling Spirit of Jesus
and living with the guidance of God.

I am alive with an awareness of God's presence in all of creation
and living in a world of possibilities.

I am alive with a faith that does not rely on the material things
of this world
and living with an understanding of what I must do.

I am alive with a habitual awareness of His presence
and living authentic relationships with others.

I am alive with a soul that is refreshed with God's forgiveness
and a life that is grounded in His love.

I am alive with absolute confidence that everything will be okay
and living in anticipation of something new.

I am alive with an enduring awareness of His presence in my life
and living with a well-placed sense of loyalty to Jesus.

Being alive is wonderful.
Being alive with Christ is even better.
Lord Jesus, allow me to always say,
"I am alive with the life of Christ."

Below is a simple prayer that I had written 10 years before
having my stroke. I think you will appreciate why it is my new

favorite prayer. A week after my stroke, I began to actually hear my pulse in my right ear. It is most noticeable when I lay down in bed at night. When I first become aware of the whooshing sound, I was concerned that it was indicative of something medically wrong. When the doctors said not to worry, that it wasn't that uncommon, I became annoyed. I did not like this foreign sound. My attitude changed when I came across my prayer:

HEARTBEAT

You are the ultimate heart specialist, Lord.
Make Your heart one with my heart.
Create for me a new identity
so full of life that two hearts beat as one.
Permit the sound of two hearts to be as one.
Permit the love of two hearts to be as one.

Now whenever I hear my pulse, I recall one line in my prayer, "Permit the sound of two hearts to be as one." Many years earlier, while in dialogue with Jesus, I asked Him to "Make Your heart one with my heart." It is such a delightful sound.

THE FOUR CATALYSTS FOR DIALOGUE PRAYER

Life is a springboard for prayer. In retrospect, I've discovered the four catalysts for dialogue prayer:

- **Imagination** — thinking about the life of Christ
- **Ordinary circumstances** — everyday life events

- **Reflection** — the outcome of quiet prayer and awareness of the presence of God
- **Random** — thoughts that just come to mind that are converted to prayer

I'm a big fan of Blessed Mother Teresa. When I heard her conclude a talk with this statement, "Do small things with great love," it inspired me to write a prayer. It seems that we Americans must measure success, and then we seek recognition for it. The accomplishments of some people are newsworthy, and we hear all about them. But what about the people who simply fulfill their family obligations, who set an example for their children that is grounded in spiritual values? We never hear about all the people who do good deeds and go unnoticed. Their accomplishments do not make the headlines, yet their impact is of lasting value, and their contribution to the spiritual well-being of others is immeasurable:

SMALL THINGS

The world does not see me in quiet moments of prayer, Lord.
The world does not witness my little acts of love.
The world is not impressed.
But it means something to You, Lord,
and it means something to other souls.
And that is all the recognition I will ever need.
Help me to do small things with great love.
Your love.

The true standard for success was set for us in Nazareth by the Holy Family. Joseph, the man who adopted the Christ child, proved his stewardship by providing for the family. Mary, a stay-at-home mom, lived a humble life doing the mundane housework while raising Jesus.

Imagining the life of Mary is illuminating. She was a young woman of great courage. She had the most important influence on the humanity of her Son, Jesus. Because of my own mother, I can identify with the nurturing and guiding qualities of Mary. I understand a mother's love and the irreplaceable mother-son relationship.

By imagining Mary in her role as mother, I can relate to her difficulties and her desires. She did not know what to expect, from one day to the next. But in all of Christianity, it is Mary who gives us the one example of perfect faith:

MOTHER MARY

Dear Blessed Mother Mary,
help me understand
what a mother
wants for her Son.
Dear Jesus,
help me understand
what a Son
wants for His mother.

The household of the Holy Family is a great place to visit in your imagination. They were hidden. During their lifetime, they received no publicity or recognition. Yet they set the standard against which every family can be measured.

Family gatherings are times for gratitude; they are occasions to say, "Thank you, Jesus." We are truly blessed with four children, three sons-in-law, and seven grandchildren. It makes for a full house when we are all together. It was after family gatherings that I wrote this prayer:

FAMILIA

Please join us, Lord, as we gather around
the kitchen table this evening.
Everyone at the table is related.
We are children and grandchildren,
wives and husbands,
daughters and sons,
sisters and brothers.
We are united by marriage
and something stronger:
the love You taught us to share.
When we are together, there is a
special happiness sensed by everyone present.
It is a good family and we all feel at home.
We savor these times.
Isn't that how you planned it, Lord?
You imagined families
gathered around the kitchen table
and each member
thinking of himself or herself
as one of the family.
Your family.

Pam and I dedicated a fair amount of time working with troubled teens. Years ago, when we lived in Denver, we were both matched up in a one-to-one relationship with teenagers through a program called Partners. The Partners program is modeled after Big Brothers/Big Sisters — however, the kids accepted into the program are referred by the juvenile court and school counselors. They are not in serious trouble for criminal behavior, but these kids come with a label attached: "At-Risk Youth."

Our experience in Denver taught us about the positive influence adults can have on teens. For the most part, these are teens who are acting out as a way to get attention; they are children, really — individuals who need guidance. Four years later, we started a Partners branch in the San Francisco Bay Area. With Pam's support, and our joint commitment, I spent five years getting the program going. When I left, our very first employee, Becky Cooper, took over the program. It was spun off from Partners in Denver and renamed Friends for Youth. Under her leadership, the program has flourished, and over 1,650 teens have been matched with adults. This prayer comes from the experience of working with teenagers:

TEENAGERS

One teen questioned his self-worth,
another said she felt empty.
They had all the material things they could ever want,
and were unfulfilled.
I told them about You and how You felt about them.
Each one a blessing.
Each one a unique creation.
Each one a part of Your plan.
Each one sacred.
I told them to fill the empty space with You.

When they did that
they had all the spiritual things they could ever want,
and were fulfilled.
After that, no words were spoken,
but You knew what
was in their hearts . . .
because You were there.

For Catholics, all prayer draws us to the Eucharist. We desire to receive Our Lord in the fullest way possible. As I learned to pray the Mass, I begin to comprehend its mystery and the manner in which the Last Supper is made present today:

THE FIRST LOAF

In my imagination
I am with a group of my closest friends.
We are gathered around the dinner table
and there is excitement in the air.
This is unlike any other meal.
Jesus is our host.
History will record this banquet
as the Last Supper.
I visualize Jesus holding a flat, round loaf of bread.
He holds it up for all of us to see.
"Take and eat," He says,
"this is My body, given up for you."
And the bread, that first loaf, becomes holy.
My mental picture ends and
I am brought back to the reality of the present.

At this moment I am actually
walking down the aisle
having just received Holy Communion.
Lord, You broke the bread.
You shared it with your disciples.
And today, You continue breaking the bread.
Once again, You are present.
Once again, the bread is made holy.
Once again, it is shared with Your friends.
Jesus, You made it easy to imagine
the Last Supper,
because I feel like
I've been there before.

After the crucifixion of Jesus, the two disciples on the road to Emmaus were so preoccupied with their own grief and uncertainty that they failed to recognize the resurrected Christ. It is only in the breaking of the bread that "their eyes were opened" (Lk 24:31). Today, it is in receiving the Eucharist that your eyes will be opened, and that God's mysteries will be illuminated:

LUMINA

Light symbolizes hope, power, and deliverance.
Light makes things visible.
St. Paul recognized You in a blinding light.
Angels are depicted in light.
We are told to obey Your commandments and walk in light.
You, Jesus, are the Light of the world.
Today, I pray that I may realize Your presence in my life.
It is You, Jesus, who makes the truth visible.

Help me, Jesus, to see the light.
Your Light.

On one occasion while I was kneeling at prayer, I noticed that my hands were cupped as they would be if I wanted to fill them with water from a faucet. My empty hands were not folded together in the usual manner of prayer:

EMPTY HANDS

Lord, as I kneel in prayer today
I am not holding my hands
in the usual way.
My hands are cupped together,
empty and ready for Your love
to be poured into them.
I've been praying in gratitude for gifts You have given me
and wondering what I have to give You in return.
But, Lord, I come up empty handed.
What do I have that can be of value to You?
Take my empty hands.
Become my empty hands.
Reach others with my empty hands.
My hands are empty, Lord,
and I welcome You to fill them.
This is all I have, Lord,
empty hands.

In the Eucharist, the unseen reality of unity is taking place. Neither the fact that we attend Mass nor the process of walking up the aisle with others to receive Holy Communion unifies us. It is the content of the host — Jesus — Who creates unity. The symbols of unity pass away, but the unseen presence of Jesus remains:

THE BODY OF CHRIST

With Jesus dwelling within me
I become part of His body,
I strengthen His Body,
I enable His work to carry on
in a way that it will not otherwise continue.
Without my willing participation
His body is weakened,
His body lacks the ability
to nourish others through me.
Without me,
the unique work I am called upon to perform
will go to someone else.
May I always say, "Yes!"
May I awaken to awareness
of Your indwelling presence like never before.
Without my response, the Body of Christ is incomplete.
For a Christian,
the formation of the Body of Christ
is the opportunity of a lifetime.
It is a challenge and a grace.
Each day we are given a sacred choice.
And I pray for all of us
that we will have the courage to say, "Yes!"

Every day, my friend and spiritual director, Father Vito Perrone, spends many hours in prayer. Much of his time is spent in quiet solitude. I dedicate this prayer to him:

A SYMPHONY IN SILENCE

In the quiet hour of prayer
I listen for the sound of Your voice.
Today I reflect on the Incarnation.
Jesus, how can I possibly help You?
Who am I to complete the work of Your Incarnation?
It hurts me to think of how much I lack.
How can I lead people to You?
I am not a preacher, Jesus.
I am not a minister, Jesus.
I am a simple person.
I lead a simple life.

A symphony interrupts my quiet thoughts.
Is that You, Jesus?
Your love is the string section.
Your hope is the winds.
Your percussion section awakens me.
The sounds are harmonious.
You are playing the music I enjoy.
It is Your music and it reminds me:
You were a simple person.
You led a simple life.

I'll take You with me today, Jesus.
And You can love my small circle

of family,
co-workers,
and friends
through me.

Once again it is time for silence.
The Master Conductor has lifted His baton.
The overture is starting
and I must pick up my bow.
What piece will we play today?

I have found that the most notable characteristic of the unseen power of prayer is the constant desire for more. The cup fills ever so slowly — and no matter where we are in the process, there is a longing for knowledge and for intimacy. We converse with Jesus only to find the dialogue incomplete. We come back again and again. Each experience draws us closer, but we never arrive. The joy we experience is derived from His presence along the way:

INSATIABLE APPETITE

Were we created
with an insatiable appetite
for holiness?
for wisdom and understanding?
for love?
Some questions are profound —
they seem unanswerable,
and yet
we continue to ask.

Lord, did You create us
with this insatiable appetite
. . . and will it
ever be satisfied?

    I can identify with inactive Catholics, people who elect to stay away from the Catholic Church. Frankly, I've been there. The rationales I hear from inactive Catholics today include the obvious issues: they reject the institution; they are angry about flawed leadership and the sins of priests; and they discard teaching that they consider to be out of step with modern society, teachings that are out of sync with their behavior:

JESUS THE LIBERATOR

Jesus, I pray
for my friends who
have become estranged from the Church,
and estranged from You.
Some pretend to be agnostic.
They delude themselves.
A few are even hostile.
Their anger is misplaced.
They feel alienated
and they have withdrawn.
A vacuum has been created.
They want their freedom.
They are hostage to their anger.
They don't understand, Lord,
that You are the divine liberator.
It is You Who came to

lead all of us to spiritual freedom.
Lead my friends back
to friendship with You.

Some inactive Catholics are searching in earnest for the truth. We welcome their return, just as Jesus welcomed us. We flawed people stick together as we try to find our way. The apostle Thomas asked Jesus directly, "How can we know the way?" Jesus replied, "I am the way, and the truth, and the life; no one comes to the Father, but by me" (Jn 14:5, 6). Lord, have mercy, and forgive us for the times we have failed to abide by Your words:

MERCY

Lord, have mercy on us, for taking You for granted.
Lord, have mercy on us, for our ingratitude.
Lord, have mercy on us, for our uncharitable conversations.
Today, we recommit ourselves to paying attention to Your way.
We recommit ourselves to recalling Your lessons.
We recommit ourselves to appreciating why
You came into this world, and what You did for each one of us.
We recommit ourselves to reciprocating the love You have given us.
And we beg Your mercy on our disrespectful actions,
our failure to love You,
and our contemptible ingratitude.
Lord, have mercy.

Faith is a free gift from God. At times, I have accepted it. At times, I have walked away. I have learned that it takes courage to accept faith because it comes with responsibilities attached. It is the more difficult choice because of the unknown demands that await the person of faith. Rejection is the easier choice, but it leads to spiritual starvation.

It pains me to recall the role of a false witness in *The Passion Play*, which I played in college. There is no prayer that digs deeper into my emotional depths than reflecting on the Passion of Christ: the Passover meal, the institution of the Eucharist, saying good-bye to friends, the sorrowful farewell to Mary, the prayers in the garden, the arrest and mistreatment, the confrontation with arrogant judges, the whipping, the false witnesses, the final judgment, the embarrassment, the torture of carrying the cross, the nails, the duration on the cross, His death, the tomb, and finally His resurrection.

Under Roman law, scourging was used as a punishment in preparation for execution. The whip, made of leather straps with metal attached to the ends, was designed to tear the flesh. This form of punishment was often fatal. We do not know the number of lashes inflicted on Jesus. We do know that for anyone of us, scourging would be unbearable:

I'm Sorry I Hurt You

We don't know the number of lashes You received, Lord.
A single lash is too much.
I cannot imagine being the one to tear Your flesh.
I've never used a whip, Lord, but I know I have hurt You.
I didn't tear your flesh, Lord, but I broke Your heart.
I hurt You when I failed to love.
I hurt You when I failed to forgive.
I hurt You when I forgot to say, "Thank you."
I hurt You when I got too busy to include You in my life.

I've punished You, Lord.
And I've punished myself.

Jesus received the death penalty of crucifixion. It was considered a deterrent to crime because it was such a severe form of punishment. The Roman custom was for the dagger-shaped cross, or just the crossbeam, to be carried by the criminal to the place of execution. The criminal was stretched out on the cross, and the hands were fastened with nails. It was the custom to use rope to prevent the body from coming loose. Nails alone would not support the weight of the body. After the cross with the person's body fastened to it was raised to the upright position, the feet were nailed in place. I get sick just thinking about it.

Jesus was offered a narcotic drink to numb the pain, but He refused it. When I read in our creed that Jesus suffered and died, it is easy to gloss over the "suffered" part. It is even more difficult to relate to the severity of His suffering. The sound of His body — the holy body of Jesus — being pierced with nails is almost incomprehensible. The severity of His suffering is unthinkable because I don't want to think about it:

THIRSTY

Did You wish for something cold to drink when You cried out,
"I thirst!"
or was it a different kind of thirst You wished to quench
when You were on the cross?
Did You thirst for souls?
Did You thirst for souls willing to unite their lives,
their sufferings, with Yours?

Were You seeking a different kind of refreshment?
I don't think You were asking for something cold to drink, Lord.
You thirst for dedication and commitment.
You thirst for souls who recognize the greatest gift of love
ever given.
I also thirst, Lord. I thirst for the courage
to become all You want me to be,
all I can possibly be . . . for You.
You alone can satisfy my thirst.
May I in some small way satisfy Yours?

The life of Christ did not end on Good Friday. He is alive!

He Is Risen

Like the two disciples
on the road to Emmaus
I am confused and amazed.
I have been on my road
searching for answers,
looking for signposts,
looking for directions,
looking for You.
My road leads me
to the doorsteps of Your home,
the Church.
I'm beginning to understand.
It is in receiving You
in the banquet of the Eucharist,
the Bread of life,
that the road shines with directions

so clear that I cannot fail to find my way.
The road to Emmaus is my road, too.
It always leads to You.
You are the Risen Christ.
You are risen in me.
We travel the road together.
In You, all of life
becomes focused.
For this moment, Lord,
the search for You has ended
for I can say,
"The Risen Lord dwells within me."

Through the writings of Cora Evans, I've learned that Christ's joy on earth is "to relive His resurrection in souls." This prayer reminds me to be aware of His presence every day:

You Should See What I Saw

Today I saw the sunrise.
I saw my wife awaken to a new day.
I saw my dog's tail wag as if to say, "Good morning."
I saw people in line for coffee at Starbucks.
I saw a beggar's home made out of cardboard.
I saw workers on a new building site.
I saw other workers and looked directly into their eyes.
I saw a few of my children
and their children, too.
And tonight
as I close my eyes
I recall that I invited You

to relive Your Mystical Humanity through me today.
And I know some of the things You saw.
Because I was there
and so were You.

True love of Jesus is the foundation for our contemplation of Christ. I pray for the grace of this kind of love. One form of contemplation is to imagine how Jesus felt. For example, imagine how His eyes felt when He cried, or imagine how His tears felt on His face:

THE TEARS OF CHRIST

Your tears feel cool on my face.
Is that how we've become . . . cool?
Have we turned away from
the warmth of Your love?
I can understand how You feel.
I can understand why You cry.
O tears of Christ, wash away our sin of indifference.
O tears of Christ, splash us — awaken us —
to Your ever-present love.
In our time of prayer let us all imagine
the tears of Christ forming in our eyes.
And please, Lord, with our love,
may we wipe away
Your tears.

I am grateful that one outcome of my stroke is tears; my right eye seems to have an overactive tear duct. Often the tears become a random reminder of the tears of Jesus and reawaken me to His indwelling presence. Little did I know that something far more serious was going on, and that I would soon experience the meaning of unity in Christ as never before.

CHAPTER SEVEN

Recognize the Source of Unity

"I heard His loving voice through the other people and came to a deeper awareness of how much He wants me to allow Him to work through me. What a gift . . . to see Jesus alive in our neighbors and to feel His abiding presence within me. He was as human as all of us and had the same way of life as the people in His world at the time. Therefore, though His experiences were different, they were as human as mine are right now. It is eye-opening and very fulfilling. The retreat helped me understand the humanity of Jesus."

RETREAT PARTICIPANT

In bold type, the newspaper headline declared: "Study calls prayer for sick people ineffective." The 2006 article in the *Washington Post* reported that praying for other people is ineffective, according to the then largest ($2.4 million) and best-designed research study examining the power of prayer. The article was picked up by newspapers across America. Results of the study became a feature story on the networks and cable television.

The article emphasized that two out of the three researched groups that were praying for heart patients were

Catholic. One statement was especially insulting: "Skeptics said the study should put to rest the notion that distant prayer has any effect." It upset me because I was at the midway point in writing my book about prayer, and neither the researchers nor the news reporters had a grasp of the true meaning of prayer. In fact, their stories revealed a complete lack of understanding, especially of the Catholic perspective.

What if the majority of their audience agreed with the study's findings? Had the researchers been able to include my recent experience at the prestigious Stanford Medical Center it would have broadened their preconceived idea of prayer and its unseen power. Here is my story.

FEAR

My wife, Pam, and our three daughters — Amy, Lisa, and Jamie — enjoy having a "girls' night out" from time to time, to celebrate a birthday or just to have time together. On this particular Friday evening, they decided to spend the night in San Francisco, at Jamie's house. The schedule worked out well for me because I was mentally exhausted after a long day at the Stanford Medical Center Eye Clinic. I was at Stanford for a second opinion: a problem, which had been originally diagnosed as glaucoma, a serious but treatable eye disease, was reassessed by the doctors at Stanford and diagnosed as something far more serious, having to do with abnormal blood flow near the brain. The combined stress of the eye exam, viewing my MRI films, listening to a language I didn't understand — with words such as "fistula" and "shunt" — and having another CT scan caught up with me. I was emotionally drained and content to just have quiet time at home alone that night.

I was expecting the phone call from my doctor, but not my reaction to her message: "The CT scan confirmed my diagnosis. There is a blunting [clot] — the blood flow is not perfect. The next step is the procedure. This is an exceedingly rare condition, but don't worry, I'll send you to the right people [doctors] — they are world-class in the field." When I connected this information with her reference to neurosurgery earlier that day, it scared me.

This was a fear I had never experienced. In the past, I never feared death. I treated death as a subject that I knew something about. I had been present when other people had passed away. I firmly believed our Catholic teachings that my soul will live with God in eternal life. On this night, however, I was dealing with emotions, not intellect. I was faced with a medical condition completely out of my control — a condition that was treatable, but with frightening risk factors. In my case, the risk was another stroke or even death. Thinking about the latter possibility caught up with me. The odds of a successful outcome were in my favor. Nonetheless, I was struck to the core of my being with the notion that I might be experiencing the prelude to my own demise.

I thought about the stories told to me by retreatants: the parents who told me about their child's life-threatening illness, the woman with a brain tumor, the woman with MS who was about to undergo open-heart surgery, the man who was going blind, and all the others. I thought of my cousin, Gaybe Lien, who was about to undergo a procedure for breast cancer when she was told that she also had lung cancer. There were so many retreatants asking for prayers. Now, for the first time in my life, I could identify with the highest level of loneliness and fear brought on by life-threatening uncertainty.

It is precisely because I felt the loneliness and fear that I am now able to identify with the feelings of others. In the garden, Jesus experienced this loneliness, just the same as me. He understands how I felt, and how you feel, because in His humanity He felt that way, too. Imagine our Creator taking on the fullness of our humanity and allowing Himself to experience human suffering, sorrow, sacrifice, and fear. As we face various trials in life, let us not forget that He is right there beside us. He has been there before, and He identifies with us.

When Jesus was suffering His agony in the garden, He pleaded with the Father: "Remove this chalice from me." Then He set the example for all time, by adding: "Not my will, but yours, be done" (Lk 22:41).

And that's how it is in life. We give ourselves totally to God, and surrender ourselves to His will.

COURAGE

As I reflect back on that time in my life, these thoughts come to mind:

> *There are three reasons why I do not want to die right now. First, I do not want to hurt Pam. Second, I want to be there for my children and their families. Third, I have work to do. It is God's work, and so much would be left undone. I feel that I would be letting Our Lord down.*

Our retreat blessing comes into play here: "May God bless you with all the desires of the eternal Father, and bless the wishes of your soul." The end of life is all about the desires of the eternal Father. Only God is indispensable. We proceed, not knowing the day or the hour (see Mt 25:13). What we do know is far more important: Jesus is right here, right now. He is not some far-off figure. He is the Risen Christ. Let us all pray for the courage to embrace the prayer of Jesus: "Not my will."

PRESENTATION OF THE GIFTS

As a couple, living in anticipation of a significant health risk, Pam and I could not have felt closer to each other. Over the years of our marriage, we have been reminded of our three-way love, with Christ as the glue bonding us. Now we were being asked to place complete trust in Him, regardless of the outcome. Sunday Mass, two days prior to the surgery, turned out to be tailor-made for us. On this day (16th Sunday in Ordinary Time, Year C), the Prayer Over the Gifts put the Mass in the context of our experience:

> Lord,
> bring us closer to salvation
> through these gifts which we bring in your honor.
> Accept the perfect sacrifice you have given us,
> bless it as you blessed the gifts of Abel.
> We ask this through Christ our Lord.

I thought about the gift of Abel. He offered the very best he had to offer in praise and worship to God.

Pam and I carried the gifts to the altar. Neither one of us could remember ever being asked to carry the gifts before. But on this day we were asked to do so as we entered church. When the time came, I carried the pitcher of wine (which "earth has given"), and Pam carried the hosts (which "human hands have made").* As we stood waiting for the priest to come down from the altar to receive the gifts, I felt a strong sense of anticipation. The gifts were about to be transformed by the Eucharistic Prayer; we were about to be transformed by receiving Jesus in the Eucharist. We were about to "share in the divinity of Christ, / who humbled himself to share in our humanity."

Back at the pew, our unspoken prayer connected our hearts with His Sacred Heart as we placed the experience in His hands. We offered ourselves, and the uncertainty we faced, as our personal gifts to Him. Prayer is always an act of faith, "the assurance of things hoped for, the conviction of things not seen" (Heb 11:1).

Later that day, I received the Anointing of the Sick. I was as spiritually prepared as possible.

COMPLETE TRUST

On the morning of the surgery, a message of absolute trust arrived from dear friends, John and Maribeth Rodee:

> We've asked God's blessing on you, those treating you today and in thanksgiving for your complete and speedy recovery. Our prayers are answered, will continue to be answered, always are, always will be.

UNITY

The procedure was a complete success. Thank God for vascular surgery, micro-medical devices, and highly skilled neuro-

---

* In the early history of the Church, the gifts included water, wine, bread, and foodstuffs for the poor. Today the monetary donations collected by the ushers are often placed near the altar. In some Catholic parishes, the entire congregation walks to the sanctuary and places the gifts of foodstuffs for the poor near the altar.

surgeons. Without this procedure, I would have lost all sight in my right eye, and the problem would have continued unabated.

Many people prayed for me, for our family, and for the doctors. There were prayer groups, announcements at Mass, a Cursillo team, and families — many people I don't even know were saying prayers. As I thought about this, I realized that Drew and Cyndi Peterson in Solano Beach, California, don't know Al and Gina Barber in New Canaan, Connecticut; Al and Gina don't know Jo Ann and Rob Smith in Glendale, California; Jo Ann and Rob don't know Doreen and Dan James in Foster City, California; and Doreen and Dan don't know Irene and Mark Montgomery... and so it goes in many locations across the country. And the common thread that connected each one is prayer — an act of faith.

Imagine all the people in this circle of prayer connected — and they *are* connected. This is the Mystical Body of Christ in action. Many spiritual writers drop the word "mystical" when referring to the Body of Christ; however, it remains a profound mystery — embraced only by faith. Let us pray for one another, that we may all come to a better understanding of the unity we share in Christ, and that we may understand His love so that we may love Him more, and be ever grateful for our connection with one another through Christ.

We must pray for people who suffer: they endure actual pain. Pray for people in sorrow: they experience grief. Pray for those who sacrifice: they do for others. Perhaps the circumstances of your life have you in special need of prayers right now. Jesus allows you to share His cross and lift His burden by uniting your suffering, sorrow, and sacrifice to Him. Imagine being able to lift even some small part of the burden Jesus experienced during His earthly time. Jesus is the great respecter of wills. All it takes is your intention to freely offer the circumstances of your life to Him. Imagine the eyes of Christ looking at you in appreciation for your great gift to Him. At times, when we experience great suffering and sorrow, the question becomes "Where is God in all this?" When we unite ourselves with Jesus in prayer, we are consoled by His answer.

How do we respond to the $2.4 million research study that concluded that praying for other people is ineffective? Our response must come in the form of prayer. Pray that the people involved in the study and those influenced by its findings will come to understand the unseen power of prayer. Pray that they will come to know the unity we share.

Life may be a time of passing, but there is never a moment when we are disconnected from eternal life. From the very beginning when we are given our soul (which we believe happens in the womb), we are drawn forward by the grace of God, with the ability to respond, the desire to find our true self, and the awareness that at the core of our discovery within is Christ Himself.

I no longer view my life so much as a journey *toward* God, but as a prayer *with* God. There will always be tensions, the realities of worldly stress, the interest in sports, the desire for entertainment, and the joy of family. These natural aspects of life fit into the journey mode, for which we allocate time. Time passes. Experiences change. Life, however, is about today. The power you have is the power of Christ within you at this moment. You are not preparing for prayer; you are living it.

Here is the response to Psalm 138 at the Sunday Mass following my surgery: "Lord, on the day I called for help, you answered me."

CHAPTER EIGHT

Trust Jesus

"In my discussion group, a lady's son was in an accident four years ago. He ended up in ICU for 2 weeks, and she prayed the hardest she had ever prayed during that time. At the end of the 2 weeks, he died. She felt abandoned and wondered what else God could want from her. She felt so much pain, unbearable pain and loneliness, for the first 24 hours. Until she looked at a crucifix. She saw all the pain in Jesus' face and realized that He has suffered so much more than she has. She then prayed to Him to get her through this time. She looks back now and believes it was a miracle that she is where she is today. She said her family "got exactly what we needed." She has a much stronger faith now, and her family is able to laugh again and talk about her son with smiles. I will take this story with me for the rest of my life. No matter what obstacles life may have for me, Jesus will help get me through them, and it is His indwelling in me that can enable me to get others through their tough times."

RETREAT PARTICIPANT

I believe that when people live each day aware that Jesus is dwelling within them, it changes everything. Awareness of His presence draws people to the Eucharist, and it fosters the desire to develop an ever deeper, heartfelt relationship with Him. The Eucharist is the source of the most intimate union possible with Christ. That is why Pope Benedict XVI calls the Eucharist "the heart of life."

With the Eucharist, our faith grows and we are enlightened. It happens over time. The closer we come to Our Lord, the more clarity we have about how we can best participate in His mission. Before long, we take ownership and realize that His mission is accomplished through us. Then we move forward with confidence.

With jobs, responsibilities raising children, and car pools and appointments, the majority of Catholics cannot receive the Eucharist more than once, maybe twice, a week. In his 2003 encyclical letter, *Ecclesia de Eucharistia* (On the Eucharist in its Relationship to the Church, no. 34), Pope John Paul II referred to "spiritual communion" as an important way of prayer. My mother taught me about spiritual communion when I was a young boy. On those days when I am unable to go to Mass and receive Jesus in the Eucharist, I can ask Him to come to me in a spiritual communion. I believe He accepts the invitation.

This is the Mystical Humanity of Christ. It is Eucharistic spirituality, and it recognizes that the work of the Incarnation continues through people who are willing to incorporate Jesus into their daily lives. This is why daily prayer and communion with God — sacramental and spiritual — are so important. Essential, really.

INSIGHT

Holy Family Elementary, Loyola High School, University of San Diego — you might think that with an all-Catholic educational background, I would fully understand the mysteries of our faith. In truth, learning is a process. We wait in anticipation of some new fragment of understanding. For Catholic priests, the Eucharist is the challenge to educate, the opportunity to nourish. For the faithful, the Eucharist drives everything, including their willingness to participate in evangelization, the courage to speak up about our Catholic faith; their involvement in ministries; their understanding of the spirituality of funding various causes; and their efforts to encourage vocations. All of these activities find their source in the Eucharist. The decisions people make to participate are inspired by Jesus Himself.

There have been many illuminating moments, times when just the right combination of ideas provides the answer. While we are on our earthly journey, we do our best to comprehend the unknown and embrace the rest as an act of faith. That is why I often recommend that people pray for wisdom: "Jesus, help me understand Your love so that I may love You more."

TRUST

We have a tradition at our retreats of presenting the pastor, or celebrant, with a framed picture of Jesus. The "Trusting Jesus" watercolor was painted by my mother, Mary Parrish McDevitt (1909-2005). She had always wanted to paint the face of Christ, but never felt inspired to do so until returning from Mass one Sunday. She said the actual painting only took about 20 minutes. (Watercolor painting is a very unforgiving medium. You cannot go back and touch things up.)

When she was finished, she held the picture at arm's length to view it and realized for the first time that she had painted Jesus with His eyes closed. She said that Jesus trusts us so much that He can close His eyes — hence the title,

"Trusting Jesus." She also wrote a prayer, "The Lesson of Trust," to go with the painting:

THE LESSON OF TRUST

Help me, dear Lord, to cease attempting to bear the pain of the future. It seems I am always trying to jump hurdles that I fear are out there waiting for me. Help me to relax, to realize that if I attempt to jump these hurdles before I reach them, I will fall! Please give me the grace to relax and to rest my head against Your Heart, and there learn the lesson of trust.

She often reminded me that God only gives us the graces for today.

*"Trusting Jesus," by Mary Parrish McDevitt
(courtesy of the author)*

OUR FAMILY MAXIM

When I graduated from college, my mother presented me with a plaque. Engraved on the brass plate was a question inscribed in Latin: "*Quid Hoc Ad Aeternitatem?*" This was our family maxim when I was growing up. In the most difficult of circumstances, the question reminds us to approach every situation with trust: "How does it look in the light of eternity?"

JOY

This book summarizes my insights on the unseen power of prayer. There is a reason why we call our belief the Catholic faith — the operative word being "faith." You are called to embrace God with *faith*, live with a sense of *hope* that is grounded in the promise Our Lord made to you, and to express your faith by revealing your *love* for others.

I would like everyone to know that living with a heightened awareness of the living, indwelling presence of Jesus every day is a joy-filled experience. There is nothing like it. It truly becomes a way of life that places everything else — the happiness of life and the sorrows — into perspective.

In the end, we are accountable to Jesus. The question that confronts us, the question we must be prepared to answer every day is "In what way am I proving my loyalty to Jesus?" There is great joy in discovering the answer.

CHAPTER NINE

Encourage Others

"There are times in each one of our lives when we need to hear a friend's word of comfort, to see a smile of encouragement, or to receive a letter of consolation, bringing peace, joy, and love into our lives. I'm sure these letters will be a source of spiritual help, as they were for Jim Ware, providing consolation and strength to anyone who is suffering under the weight of his or her own cross."

FATHER FRANK PARRISH, S.J.

Letter writing is a lost art. This is unfortunate because writing affords you an opportunity to express yourself from the heart and allows you the time to construct just the right message. You can imagine your audience, one individual, actually hearing your words, your most heartfelt thoughts, as though you were actually saying them in person. Sending a get-well card and writing a letter are vehicles for prayers. Words of encouragement, expressed in the context of faith, place your good wishes before Jesus and allow Him to express His love through you. In this regard, I have a story to tell.

My experience of writing letters to Jim Ware was extraordinary in how it came about, emotional in the content of the messages, and inspirational in how it ended. In 1978, 14 years before Father Frank appointed me custodian of the writings of Cora Evans, I was reading Cora's book *Letter Lessons*. The book consists of 31 letters written to Father Frank. Each letter includes reflections on a Scripture passage, with Cora's commentary, suggested meditations, and an assignment to be carried out each day during the week. The idea is to read one letter a week and complete the daily tasks before reading the next letter. For me, each new letter brought a sense of eager anticipation.

The first assignment in *Letter Lessons*, written by Cora Evans 24 years earlier, ended with a call to action: "Every day for a week write a letter to a sick friend." I was at a loss how to fulfill her request. For the life of me, I could not think of a friend who was sick. Then, the very next day, I received a letter from my mother, asking me if I would write to the son of an old family friend, who was very ill. His name was Jim Ware. What an unusual coincidence — or so I thought at the time. It was during the process of writing to my new sick friend that I connected the dots. Jim Ware was Cora's godson.

This is how the dots connect: Cora became godmother for Jim in 1953. She wrote the letter lessons over a two-year period, beginning in 1954. Cora passed away in 1957 and could not have known that her suggestion of writing to a sick friend would one day be acted on for the benefit of her own godson.

DIVINE PROVIDENCE
Some dates are unforgettable. We remember them because throughout our whole life the events of the day are incomparable. And when the events are providential, we realize how

blessed we are to experience such a joy. We may even have insight into our own destiny. June 4, 1978, was like that for me: the day I began writing letters to Jim Ware, a person I did not know, but would grow to love.

In this chapter, I include excerpts from my letters to Jim. Rather than starting each subsection with the salutation "Dear Jim," as the letters began, I am making this section of the book personal. Imagine that each letter is an individual message addressed to *you*. When you see the name Jim, or the reference to friend or brother, substitute your own name.

In my first letter to Jim, I asked rhetorical questions:

Was it just some accident that I would happen to pick up Cora's *Letter Lessons*? Was it an accident that her first lesson says, "Write a letter to a sick friend?" Was it an accident that my mom wrote to me about you, and was it an accident that you are Cora's godson? Could it be, that for one or, more likely, both of us, it was no accident at all?

Today, I would answer that it illustrates the unseen power of prayer. My decision to publish these personal letters, originally intended only for Jim Ware, is based on his mother's wishes. Unknown to me at the time, Vera Ware, Jim's mom, saved all of the letters. She read them after Jim passed away and then sent them back to me, with this statement:

Maybe your holy letters can be used to help other ill people. I know that each day your letter arrived and I brought them to Jim, it was like a ray of sunshine. Jim was eager to open the letter and hear, through you, God's message for that day, and a peace would come over Jim. Your letters helped more than words can say.

Now you are the person who is receiving these messages of love and hope. It is my prayer that by sharing these letters, you will come to better understand God's way of working through people, especially through you. He wants to use each of us to reach others with His love. It is for God's glory, and in His name, that I share the Jim Ware letters with you. The headlines have been added for clarity.

CHILDREN OF LIGHT

Allow me to share with you a notion about the spiritual meaning of a rainbow.

> *"Truly, truly, I say to you, unless one is born of water and the Spirit, he cannot enter the kingdom of God." (Jn 3:5)*

> *"For once you were darkness, but now you are light in the Lord; walk as children of light (for the fruit of light is found in all that is good and right and true)." (Eph 5:8-9)*

It takes water, many tiny raindrops, and sunlight, to make a rainbow. Are we not like the raindrops — each one acting as a tiny prism and mirror to break up and reflect sunlight, His light, into colors for all to see and enjoy?

And so, Jim, with my little drawing [of a rainbow] I've started to respond to the request your godmother made January 11, 1954, and directed to me today, June 4, 1978. It is no accident. This is how God works. We never fully understand "why" or "how," but each one of us, like each raindrop in the rainbow, is necessary and important to make God's great masterpiece complete.

Peace to you, and all children of light.

OUR JOURNEY

Caterpillars go through different stages on their journey through life. And in the end they are among the most beautiful and graceful of all God's creatures.

As butterflies, they travel from flower to flower, carrying pollen from one flower to another. And from the flower they drink the sweet nectar.

It seems to me that we all begin our journey like the caterpillar. We grow to the grace and beauty of the butterfly, and then we go from one flower to another, sharing the gifts we can bring and drinking in the sweetness that is there.

Peace.

THE WAY OF SPIRITUAL LIFE

This is the way of our spiritual life: We climb and fall back, and climb a little higher. We grow in understanding, knowledge, wisdom, and faith. We find our special moments of quiet prayer and oneness with Him, but it doesn't last. And then once again we begin our climb. And each time we pray, each time we reach to God, we grow in spirit and light. But the process never ends; there is always more, as our capacity to love increases.

My prayer for today is that Our Lord will continue to bless you. Of this I am certain: He loves you. His love for you is so great, so complete, and He wants you to know that and believe it.

In prayer, ask Him to help you understand His love a little more. And today, I will do the same. So with this better understanding of love, we can love Him more.

In His love, I wish you peace.

ACCEPTANCE BY GOD

I found this part of Scripture to be beautiful and meaningful to me, and I'd like to share it with you. "Beloved, let us love one another; for love is of God, and he who loves is born of God and knows God. He who does not love does not know God; for God is love. In this the love of God was made manifest among us, that God sent his only-begotten Son into the world, so that we might live through him. In this is love, not that we loved God but that he loved us and sent his Son to be the expiation for our sins. Beloved, if God so loved us, we also ought to love one another. No man has ever seen God; if we love one another, God abides in us and his love is perfected in us" (1 Jn 4:7-12).

Certainly we understand the need for love and that we must try through our lives to love one another. This openness on our part, this willingness to love, is what brings us closer to God, "For God is love." My brother, let us take our understanding of God's love for us, God's acceptance of us as we are, and share it with each other and all others we encounter. This is not simply a good thought, John tells us, "And this commandment we have from him, that he who loves God should love his brother also" (1 Jn 4:21).

With that, my feelings for you and our relationship are expressed.

Peace.

EXPERIENCE HIS PRESENCE

Cora wrote, "Let us, through the knowledge of tradition, study of Scripture and obedience to the voice of the Church, outgrow the cloak of the sparrow and rise into the strength of the eagle. A sparrow's morning flight is to the ground searching for food. The eagle rises into the eons before he eats and soars into the brightness of the rising sun. Often he rises above the clouds and then returns only when the atmosphere is too thin for survival. Do we follow the eagle? Do our souls rise for moments, upon rising, to the limits of our strength to the SON? To do so is to build a firm foundation of faith."

In the same Letter Lesson, written in 1954, Cora speaks to those who are ill. Perhaps this has special meaning for you: "Detachment … is not to pray particularly for self and trouble, but for all the people suffering from the same condition." Cora continues with this thought for mothers praying for their children: "When our child is ill, do we forget all the other sick children? Broaden that river of grace and in a spirit of detachment pray for all sick children, for many do not have mothers of faith to pray for them, and your prayers will be heard, for God will not be outdone in generosity. Let us become generous with self and others."

My spiritual brother, I am with you in quiet prayer. It is in His peace that I have come to know and love you. We, my family and I, pray for you, and as Cora asks, for all the others.

May you feel His peace, and may you experience His presence. Become the Eagle!

The previous letter, dated October 23, 1978, was my last letter to Jim Ware. Jim passed away three days later.

I received the following letter from Jim's mother about six months after he passed away.

A Letter From Jim's Mother

Dearest Mike, Pam and your precious family,

Thank God, Mike, I have all the letters you were so Christ-like to write to Jim. The letters were a very personal thing with Jim; he did not share them with me and I never even gave it a thought, as he had been completely on his own, away from "Mother's apron strings" for over four years. Sharing letters from a friend with Mom was not thought of, even during his stay here with me from the last of April until God called him "Home" the last of October.

The last letter, Mike — I feel Cora knew and inspired you to write that letter to Jim, as it is such a tremendous, beautiful letter. Your letters helped more than words can say. God bless you.

Jim told me, as he sat on that bed, he never, ever in all his life felt the presence of Our Lord like he did that morning (his hospital bed after receiving the Eucharist). In coming home from the hospital a short time after that, he read your letter and said, "I do not know Mike McDevitt by face, but, Mom, I felt his presence beside me, here on this sofa, just the same as if he were sitting here in person, talking with me as I read his letter."

Jim also mentioned you, Pam, and the children, after reading the letters. All of you were close, dear friends, just as you still are to Jim. I hope by returning these letters I have fulfilled your wish, Mike.

Have a glorious Easter.

Gratefully,
Vera Ware
Mother of Jim Ware

When Jim told his mother that he could feel my presence as he read one of my letters, he was describing the unseen presence through which we are all connected.

When you write to a sick friend, and your message is grounded in faith, you connect with that person soul to soul. Your encouraging words penetrate far deeper than a slap on the back or a motivation speech. The very meaning of spirituality comes alive, because you allow Jesus to express His love through you. And you will always have the joy of knowing that the recipient got the message — the real message.

SPECIAL DEDICATION

This chapter, "Encourage Others," is dedicated to nine people who died at an early age. One, my brother Frankie, was 5 years old. My younger brother, Anthony, died in the womb. The other children range up to age 29. Age has little meaning to their parents, siblings, and friends. Nothing is as difficult as a parent's loss of a child. Nothing. And yet, in spite of their loss, or perhaps because of it, the parents (and siblings and friends) have found hope. In addition to Frankie and Anthony, this chapter is in loving memory of Tommy Kennington, Suzy Kuster, Colleen McNamara, Joey Millett, Sarah Russell, Casey Turturici, Jim Ware, and all the others — the children you know. To each one, I say: "Now you are the fledglings whose morning has come."

BECOME THE EAGLE

Every morning the Eagle soars
to meet the rising sun,
into the eons,

with brightness of spirit,
where the feelings of freedom
know no boundaries, or doors.

It is his habit, each morning, to fly at will,
to care less for caring,
to live, to fly,
and to sing,
where all feelings are free
and motion is quiet, yet nothing stands still.

Even the fledgling is off in flight,
it is morning's new habit,
and he is rising
into eons of freedom
to follow the eagles,
his spirit relaxing and touching the sight.

Now you are the fledgling whose morning has come,
feel the freedom and
fly to the Spirit
and become the Eagle.
This is your morning,
so soar to the eons and fly to the Son.

(Dedicated to all the fledglings.)

I received one letter from Jim. It bears witness to the impact you can have when you write words of encouragement to a sick friend.

THE LETTER FROM JIM WARE

Greetings Spiritual Brother,

Well, I have finally got myself in gear in order to respond to such nice mood-breaking and thought-inspiring letters. It's always great to receive one of your letters, as the thoughts that are running through them are mine for the day as well. Cora must be working overtime. For not knowing you personally, or your family, I feel as though there is a strong and sincere bond between us that will only grow stronger each day. The love of God draws all men together, but it seems to have stronger bonds between certain individuals.

My friend, I hope that you will try to understand some of this. Cora must know and have some great influence as well as Christ Himself. Like Cora said, silent prayer is the best. I find it the best pain pill I have.

I think Pearl Bailey sums it up best. She finished her semester with four B's and an A in religion. When school officials asked for Miss Bailey's reaction, she said, "As long as you have A's with God, honey, that's all that matters!"

In my prayers,
Jim

How appropriate that Jim would sign off with "In my prayers."

ENCOURAGE OTHERS

Every single act of encouragement, no matter how small it may seem to you, moves the world closer to accomplishing Jesus' mission. The encouraging words Jesus has for others is spoken in your voice and written in your hand.

CHAPTER TEN

Pray Always

"This retreat reminds me of the saying 'So much to do, and so little time.' I feel that my role may be small, but it is all part of God's plan. I will make sure that I invite Jesus along for the ride."

RETREAT PARTICIPANT

Reading the juxtaposition between something Jesus said, "Apart from me you can do nothing" (Jn 15:5), and Paul's statement, "I can do all things in him who strengthens me" (Phil 4:13), we realize that we are not alone in our strategy to bring souls to Christ. Jesus is with us through His indwelling grace and through the resources of the Catholic Church.

SERVANTS OF CHRIST

It seems that we can view the Church along two tracks that are parallel and yet spiritually integrated. On one track, we have the Pope and the bishops as successors to the apostles, and their teaching authority (the Magisterium), which was instituted by Christ and is guided by the Holy Spirit. The view of this track includes the sacraments and the familiar organization structure. The view from the other track is quiet different.

If we could view the spirituality of the Catholic Church through the lens of the soul, the image would be inverted. Unlike the typical organization chart, with leaders at the top, these people would be at the bottom. Jesus turned everything upside down. He came to render service (see Mt 20:28 and Mk 10:45). In the salvation-of-souls business, the true spiritual leaders are servants to others, which is why Pope Benedict XVI calls himself the "Servant of Servants of God."

In the Catholic Church, men and women who offer their lives to God do so in order to be of service to the rest of us. Their dedication is founded on the conviction that they may be able to assist you in accomplishing the mission given to you by Jesus. Most often, the response of others to their efforts is unknown to them, which makes their service all the more deserving of respect.

The most important decision for these dedicated servants — choosing their vocation — came after careful and prayerful discernment. They responded to God's will by making a life-changing decision. Today their vow is apparent. The clergy and religious continue to respond to their calling by meeting the demands of personal sacrifice day after day. It is a life that places everything — their entire life and every activity along the way — in the hands of Our Lord wholeheartedly. We are privileged to have these people in our lives. They pray about their vocation, and they deserve of our prayers.

THE IMPULSE FROM CHRIST

For you and me, assuming for a moment that you are a lay person, knowing the will of God can be elusive — at least for a time. Discernment requires that you engage in prayer — or reengage, if you've disconnected yourself from God. It takes time, and you must put it all out there: your struggles, fears, and desires. You are petitioning Our Lord for guidance about how to best serve Him, given your present situation in life. In my experience, Jesus responds by providing the impulse to read and study, the incentive to have relevant discussions, and the desire to pray with greater frequency and reverence. The choices that follow, and the direction your life takes, seem so natural that you may not remember that you once prayed to know God's will. You are doing God's will, and you know it.

PEACE OF HEART

On June 4, 1982, Blessed Mother Teresa of Calcutta, founder of the Missionaries of Charity, visited San Francisco. I was fortunate to attend a private audience comprised of priests and nuns. She told us, "When Jesus said, 'My peace I leave with you, My peace I give unto you,' He was not giving a type of peace which means that we don't bother each other. He came to give the *peace of heart* that comes from loving — from serving others."

You are called to do more than say, "I love You, Jesus." You are called to fulfill your obligation to be your brother's and sister's keeper. You have an opportunity to do that every day. It does not have to be some enormous undertaking. You respond to Jesus' call when you encourage a depressed person, when you call or write a sick friend, or when you bring a hot meal to a family in need. There are many ways of bringing Jesus to people through your example. It is not about preaching; it is about doing.

Mother Teresa concluded her remarks: "The fruit of silence is prayer, the fruit of prayer is faith, the fruit of faith is love, *and the fruit of love is service.*"

A prayerful imagination can be employed to reflect on life from the vantage point of heaven. From this vista, what have you *not* done? What opportunities did you pass up that you wish you could redo? If someone in heaven asked you to tell them about your earthly life, what will you use as an example of how you praised God, glorified God, served God? Will you tell them about your role in the continuation of Jesus' life here on earth? Will you tell them that when you became aware of your body as a temple for the Holy Spirit, it changed your life? Will you talk about the way Jesus blessed others through you? And will you feel a sense of special joy because you knew you were your brother's and sister's keeper, and acted accordingly?

CHANGE THE WORLD

If there is one thing I could change in the Catholic Church today, it would be to raise expectations. The responsibility for changing the world, the challenge to bring all souls to Christ, is not someone else's job. It cannot be viewed as the task of our institutional Church. It belongs to all the faithful, and more than 98 percent of Catholics are laypeople.

The challenge is bigger today than ever before, due in large part to the number of disengaged Catholics, who, by their unwillingness to participate, are counterproductive. Their message is different than mine. By example, they say it is okay to be complacent. By action, many of them claim to be Catholic while defying fundamental doctrines of our faith. By attitude, they say the Church has serious problems — "*They* lack vocations," "*They* don't have enough priests," and "*They* lack attendance at Sunday Mass." Unknowingly, these people position themselves in an "us vs. them" relationship. How sad. There is no "they" — there is only "we." *We* Catholics lack vocations. *We* have too few priests. *We* see too few of us attending Sunday Mass. Rather than just observing serious issues facing the Catholic Church, we are all better served by addressing the question: "What am *I* doing about it?"

As I ponder our situation, two notions surface. First, there is a tension between "ability" and "willingness." When we were baptized, we became a dwelling place for the Holy Spirit — a temple — and therefore we have the ability to do something meaningful for God. The question is one of willingness. Am I willing to accept the responsibility of my faith? Am I willing to make His message my own?

FOLLOW HIS EXAMPLE

Jesus, You were humble.
Make me humble, too.
Jesus, You were brave.
Make me brave, too.
Jesus, You were hopeful.
Make me hopeful, too.
Jesus, You were peaceful.
Make me peaceful, too.
Jesus, You were joyful.
Make me joyful, too.
Jesus, I want to be
just like You.

MEMBERSHIP VS. OWNERSHIP

The second notion — the distinction between membership and ownership — is important because some Catholics confuse the two. It is true that all baptized Christians are "members" of the Body of Christ. Confusion happens when the concept of "membership" is applied to the Catholic Church, as though we all belonged to the same "club." Club membership is not a useful analogy. As a Catholic, you *own* the Catholic Church, all that it is and all that it stands for. This is no club, and none of us are on the outside looking in. We can't be. Being a critic of Church leaders and policy has its place, but it does not change the responsibility of ownership.

When Father Frank was studying to become a priest, he made a promise to Jesus: he would always say yes to every request. What a great promise! The title for my eulogy for him was obvious: "The Yes-man for Jesus." We can make the same promise. Jesus may ask the question "When you were given the chance, what did you do?"

Promise keepers will have their answer ready. Laypeople and those who are consecrated by vows and ordained ministry own the mission of Jesus. We have different roles and responsibilities. We have different opportunities, and we have been entrusted with different tasks. We proclaim the kingdom of God in different family and social settings, yet each one must say: "The mission of Jesus is my mission. His objectives are my objectives." Jesus called me His friend. He called you His friend. He didn't say that the clergy are His best friends and laypeople something less. We are friends of Jesus, and He has entrusted us to make Him visible in the world.

THE ADVERSARY

The impulse to do evil comes from the devil. Satan — formerly a heavenly leader, now also known as Lucifer and the evil one — is the prince who left his king, the King of kings, and the one who challenged the love of God when God created Adam and Eve in His image. Satan became the first adversary to rise up against God. It is Satan who spoke to Eve through the serpent. Devils are the angels of Satan.

Satan hates you and all mankind because he was expelled from heaven by Michael, the archangel who led the faithful angels. Satan, the tempter, has the unseen power to inflict evil on the spiritual life of each one of us. He disguises himself as good and promises all that the world has to offer. It is helpful to review what Scripture tells us about our adversary:

- Satan tempted Jesus (see Mt 4:1-11, Mk 1:12-13, and Lk 4:1-13).
- Satan put the idea of betraying Jesus into the heart of Judas: "The devil had already put it into the heart of Judas Iscariot, Simon's son, to betray him" (Jn 13:2).
- Satan possessed Judas: "Then Satan entered into Judas called Iscariot, who was of the number of the Twelve" (Lk 22:3).
- Satan is the master of deceit: "Peter said, 'Ananias, why has Satan filled your heart to lie to the Holy Spirit?' " (Acts 5:3).
- Satan's power over the material world is clearly expressed when he tempts Jesus: "And the devil took him up, and showed him all the kingdoms of the world in a moment of time, and said to him, 'To you I will give all this authority and their glory; for it has been delivered to me, and I give it to whom I will. If you, then, will worship me, it shall all be yours.' And Jesus answered him, 'It is writ-

ten, "You shall worship the Lord your God, and him only shall you serve" ' " (Lk 4:6-8).

St. Peter tells us we are not helpless in dealing with this opponent:

> Be sober, be watchful. You adversary the devil prowls around like a roaring lion, seeking some one to devour. Resist him, firm in your faith, knowing that the same experience of suffering is required of your brotherhood throughout the world. And after you have suffered a little while, the God of all grace, who has called you to his eternal glory in Christ, will himself restore, establish, and strengthen you. To him be the dominion for ever and ever. Amen. (1 Pt 5:8-11)

St. James the Apostle tells us how to respond to the temptation and the deceit of the devil:

> Submit yourselves therefore to God. Resist the devil and he will flee from you. Draw near to God and he will draw near to you. (Jas 4:7)

We must be in dialogue with Jesus in order to withstand the worldly temptations of our hidden adversary.

There was no ambiguity in Jesus' response to Paul:

> And the Lord said, "I am Jesus whom you are persecuting. But rise and stand upon your feet; for I have appeared to you for this purpose, to appoint you to serve

and bear witness to the things in which you have seen me and to those in which I will appear to you, delivering you from the people and from the Gentiles — to whom I send you to open their eyes, that they may turn from darkness to light and from the power of Satan to God, that they may receive forgiveness of sins and a place among those who are sanctified by faith in me." (Acts 26:15-18)

Take it from Jesus: This is no imaginary force! The Antichrist is Lucifer, the personification of the powers of evil. In the last days of earthly time, Lucifer, the Antichrist, will proclaim himself as god. Scripture tells us that many will be deceived. We must pray for all people to withstand the threat of such deception. Guard your faith. At some future time, your descendents may be among the only remaining faithful followers of Christ.

WATCH OUT FOR THE LIARS

We live in a society where there are many morally disgraceful people who call themselves spiritual mediums. They are the psychics who deceive others into believing they talk to their dead relatives. They are liars who commit the most serious sin of all. By inserting themselves between their customers and God, they guide people away from the source of hope itself. By saying, "Believe in me, believe in my version of the truth, follow me, follow my teachings," they are enemies of Jesus. Only the devil claims equality with God. Woe to anyone so deceitful.

How will they explain their contradiction to Jesus, who said, "I am the way, and the truth. . . . Follow me"? When in death they meet Jesus, will they still claim supernatural powers? Will they tell Jesus they can speak to His dead relatives? Imagine the false psychic palm reader looking at the palms of His holy and scared hands. It is a frightening image.

THE BATTLE

You are in competition against the angels of darkness. The stakes are the highest possible: your eternal soul and the souls of others who are influenced by you. In this conflict, there is no bloodshed. No lives are lost; "just" souls. We ask St. Michael the Archangel to defend us in battle, and protect us against the snares and deceptions of the devil:

> St. Michael the Archangel, defend us in battle; be our defense against the wickedness and snares of the devil. May God rebuke him, we humbly pray; and do you, O prince of the heavenly host, by the power of God, thrust into hell Satan and the other evil spirits who prowl about the world seeking the ruin of souls. Amen.

This is a prayer for world peace. In our struggle against the powers of darkness, we are assured of absolute victory by the power of Jesus' death and resurrection. His sacrifice is present at the Mass, our ultimate prayer.

THE WAY

Pray about the issues facing our Church, especially vocations to the priesthood. Live your daily life as you are, and incorporate your friend, Jesus, in every aspect of it. When you drive carpool, He will join in your laughter at the children's conversation. When you tackle frustrations, He will confront them, too. When you suffer, He will suffer through you. Become aware of His presence — and remember that Jesus, the unseen power, is within you.

THE BENEFIT

During my five-day stay in the hospital following my stroke, I thought about various recent events in my life, and the fact that I had invited Jesus to experience them with me. I discovered that it is easy to recall those times enjoyed in dialogue prayer with Him. It wasn't just about what I had experienced; it was about what the two of us had encountered. The thought made me realize that being in the hospital was something we were going through together. My mind drifted to thoughts of eternal life.

CROSSING THE BRIDGE

I know many people who are loving and compassionate and caring, who give of their time and talent for the good of others — and who do not believe as I do. In conversation, these people are accepting of my commitment to Jesus, and even of my thoughts on prayer, but they will conclude: "There are many paths." I point out that all of us, regardless of the path we have chosen, are searching for exactly the same thing. We are explorers in search of meaning. Only at the end of our earthly life will we reach the summit of our search. We will know the unknowable God, and we will see the Unseen face-to-face (see 1 Cor 13:12, Rev 22:4). Then Jesus will be revealed to us as the meaning for which we searched. This will be the fulfillment of our deepest longings.

That first night, from my hospital bed, in my imagination, I saw all paths leading to the footsteps of the bridge into heaven. No one crosses the bridge into eternal life without encountering Jesus. He is the bridge. He is the way. Many paths hold elements of the truth, but Jesus alone is the Truth of truths — the complete truth.

THE ROUNDABOUT WAY

With all the television exposure given to purported spiritual teachers, especially the ones who claim to be in touch with your dead relatives, you would think purgatory is some out-of-date concept that is no longer part of Catholic doctrine. Wrong. There is no imperfection in heaven, and purgatory is where the faithful dwell while undergoing purification. Far from being an antiquated concept, this is reality: "Death is the end of man's earthly pilgrimage, of the time of grace and mercy which God offers him so as to work out his earthly life in keeping with the divine plan, and to decide his ultimate destiny" (*Catechism of the Catholic Church*, n.1013).

This roundabout way to heaven is such a waste of time, and it is a detour you may be able to avoid. I fear purgatory because it is idle time. I fear it because I will be aware of all the false gods I put before my Lord. (I speak of the false gods of sin: self-centeredness, selfishness, greed, putting my interest and satisfaction before prayer, and the times I refused to respond to my calling.) I fear living with the blessing of salvation, but not being able to accept this remarkable gift. In my imagination . . .

I must now wait in the most monotonous circumstances, where earthly joy is but a memory and a distraction. I can't go back.

It is too late for a do-over. I am the source of my own anxiety.
This is the justice of God. No longer is there earthly time for my
prayer of petition to be said or heard. My unanswered question
is "How long will this detour last?" I fear that I am among
those in purgatory who have no family or friends who pray for
them; their prayers would give me God's blessing.

And, yet, the souls in purgatory wait in joyful hope. They
live with the certainty of arriving at their ultimate destination,
where Jesus' joy will be theirs, and their joy will be complete.

SILENT EXAMPLE OF FAITH

I would like to share my thinking about some of the most powerful people in the Church. There is nothing I know of that
compares to the example they set. I speak of the people, previ-
ously *inactive* Catholics, who have converted to be active participants in a unique way.

These are people who were inactive not because they
rejected their Catholic faith, but because they felt disfranchised
from the institutional Church. For a time, they stayed away
from the Church because of divorce and remarriage, without
receiving an annulment of the first marriage. They described
themselves as Catholic by Baptism — followers of Jesus, yet
nonparticipants. "I'm not permitted to receive the Eucharist, so
why go to Mass?" was their thinking. For the majority, the next
step was to blame the Catholic Church and look for spiritual
acceptance elsewhere. But a few of these people have become
the exception to the rule.

There are Catholics attending Mass who approach the
priest at Communion time with their hands folded across their

heart to receive a blessing — just like a child. Then, in quiet prayer, they ask Jesus to come to them in a spiritual communion. They have accepted the teachings of the Church and ask for God's merciful love (see *Catechism of the Catholic Church*, nn. 1650 and 1651). Their choice is to never be separated from Him. They show their love for God in the silent example of their faith. How blessed we are to be in the company of these wonderful souls.

If I could dare recommend one prayer for these inspirational people, it would be that they pray to receive the last sacrament, the Anointing of the Sick, when they know they are close to death. We must all pray for this grace. The *Catechism of the Catholic Church* teaches that "the Christian who unites his own death to that of Jesus views it as a step towards him and an entrance into everlasting life," with this as the "payoff": "The Church for the last time speaks Christ's words of pardon and absolution over the dying Christian, seals him for the last time with a strengthening anointing, and gives him Christ in viaticum [the Eucharist] as nourishment for the journey" (*Catechism of the Catholic Church*, n.1020). Imagine the response Jesus gives to the inactive Catholic who has chosen to pray the Mass, make spiritual communions, and engage in dialogue prayer with Him — all for the purpose of showing his or her love for Him.

LAST HOLY COMMUNION

You, as a person of faith, may experience something special when you end this earthly phase of your life. Your imagination may take you back to all the times you invited Jesus to live His resurrected life through you: the good things you did together and the times with loved ones, especially children. Perhaps you will imagine praying the Mass, walking down the aisle to receive Communion, or approaching with your hands folded across your heart to receive His blessing and make a spiritual communion. Suddenly, you realize that this is no imaginary happening. When you reach the front of the line, the priest is Christ Himself. He is offering you your last Holy Communion. You hear Him say: "Welcome home. Now, I invite you to live your resurrected life through Me."

A LIFE NOT MY OWN

We are expected to live by a set of guidelines provided by Jesus, to seek the truth, and to live according to the formation of a good conscience. We are expected to plant the seeds of spiritual growth for others, and we have been given the ability and free will to do so.

We can freely choose to incorporate Jesus into our life and give it back to Him. When we make the choice to do God's will above all else, we are living a life not our own. Life becomes a constant living in cooperation with grace. Life becomes daily prayers of inquiry: "What is Your will for me today, Lord? I invite You to relive Your Mystical Humanity, Your resurrected life, through me, beginning right now." We live with the knowledge that none other than our Lord Jesus has developed the road map for the direction we are headed. Our vision of the future becomes His vision. Our strategy for how to make that future vision a reality becomes His strategy. The goals we want to reach become His goals.

Your victory at the final hour is based on a life that is much more than your own. This is what the unseen power of prayer is all about.

The headline on the poster promoting our retreat read: "Come, follow me." Throughout Scripture, Our Lord is calling us to follow Him. Little by little, every story pulls us closer to Jesus. As we reflect on each lesson, we begin to move from examining the life of Christ to probing His messages and applying them to our life today. With the Eucharist, our faith grows and we are enlightened. It happens over time. The closer we come to Our Lord, the more clarity we have about how we can best participate in His mission.

One goal of this book is to create a heightened awareness of the living, indwelling presence of Jesus in the daily lives of the faithful. Remember the question that St. Paul posed to his followers: "Do you not know that you are God's temple and that God's Spirit dwells in you?" (1 Cor 3:16). Your affirmative answer draws you to the Eucharist, and it fosters the desire to develop an ever deeper relationship with Him. By extending the invitation to live His resurrected life, His Mystical Humanity, through you, your prayer becomes a way of living. No longer can you limit your thinking of the Catholic Church as an organization with a mission. As Cardinal Roger Mahony of Los Angeles affirmed: "It is not so much that the Church has a mission; it is rather more that the mission has a Church." This is Jesus' mission, and His mission belongs to you because you have *Him* dwelling within you.

I have a single recommendation, and it comes from the heart: Pray. Pray, and the unseen power of God will embrace and bless you, and those around you, abundantly. Pray, and you will become aware of the choices He gives you. Pray, and you will have the courage to respond to those choices. Pray, because what is unseen lasts forever.

On my desk, I have a small prayer book given to me by my parents for my first Holy Communion. The title is *Pray Always*.

Without uttering a sound today, announce to the world that you are alive with the life of Christ.

~~~

Questions for Group Discussion

QUESTIONS THAT MAY BE ASKED BY JESUS

Today you are the hands of Christ, the voice of Christ, and the eyes of Christ. Jesus wants to give His gifts to others through you. Imagine Jesus asking you these questions:

- **"When you were given the chance to help others, what did you do?"** Be specific. Describe an opportunity, the need, and how you responded. Tell how you felt and how you benefited from the experience.
- **"Can you drink of the chalice I am to drink of?"** It appears that Jesus is using the chalice as a metaphor. Discuss the meaning of His question.
- **"How have you managed the cup I have offered you?"** Describe the situation in the context of your Catholic faith.
- **"Do you love Me?"** Apparently, Jesus was not satisfied with Peter's answer. Answer Jesus' question in a way that is believable.

ADDITIONAL QUESTIONS FOR DISCUSSION

Paul asked this of his community in Corinth: "Do you not know that you are God's temple and that God's Spirit dwells in you?" (1 Cor 3:16). Father Frank said: "He died and left the world, true, but He continues to live in His resurrected life through our humanities. To me this is the very heart and apex of our Catholic faith." These beautiful teachings lead us to a spiritual-communion prayer of invitation: "Lord, I invite You to relive Your humanity, Your resurrected life, through me today." Here are some questions to ask:

- Is this a way of daily prayer for you?
- If so, how do you anticipate that it impacts your life and the choices you make?
- In what way does it change your attitude toward others?

Respond to these two questions about Jesus and Mary:

- What does Mary want for her Son?
- What does Jesus want for His mother?

As you evaluate the Catholic Church today, discuss the difference between membership and ownership, ability and willingness, community and unity:

- In what way does this discussion provide clarity and direction for you?

We know that the work of the Incarnation is still in progress and that each one of us has some small role to play:

- How do we encourage others to accept that His mission is our mission, that His objectives are our objectives?

We pray for the return of inactive Catholics:

- **What else can we do? What can you do personally?** Be specific. Make a plan. Commit to it and hold each person in your discussion group accountable. Pray about it as a group. It is not about success in terms of numbers; it is about being faithful to what we are called to do.

Discuss the habit of prayer:

- **How do you pray? When do you pray? What words do you use?**

Discuss the unseen power of prayer:

- **What does it mean to you? In what way does it have an impact on your behavior?**

APPENDIX TWO

⌇

This Book as a Prologue

Dear Reader,

When I finished writing this book, I realized that it was much more than one person's testimony. It serves as a fitting prologue to the writings of the Catholic mystic Cora Evans (1904-1957). In response to a request by her confessor and spiritual director, Father Frank Parrish, S.J., I have assumed the responsibility for the mission given to her by Our Lord: the promulgation of the Mystical Humanity of Christ throughout the world. With God's grace you will hear more about this undertaking in the future.

The Unseen Power of Prayer will have accomplished its purpose if you gain a heightened awareness of the living, indwelling presence of Jesus in your everyday life. You extend the invitation. Jesus accepts. And this new way of prayer changes your life.

I pray that this book draws you closer to Jesus, and that you have a better understanding of His personal love for you. I pray that in the process of reading and reflecting, a layer of the mystery of our faith was peeled back to give you a fresh look at the unseen power of prayer. Finally, I pray that the rest of my life will be seen by God as a single act of gratitude.

May God bless you with all the desires of the eternal Father and bless the wishes of your soul.

MICHAEL MCDEVITT
Executive Director
The Mystical Humanity of Christ, Inc.
www.ParishRetreat.org

PS: If you would like to share your story about prayer, please e-mail me at *mysticalhumanity@aol.com*.

Our Sunday Visitor ...

Your Source for Discovering the Riches of the Catholic Faith

Our Sunday Visitor has an extensive line of materials for young children, teens, and adults. Our books, Bibles, pamphlets, CD-ROMs, audios, and videos are available in bookstores worldwide.

To receive a FREE full-line catalog or for more information, call **Our Sunday Visitor** at **1-800-348-2440, ext. 3**. Or write **Our Sunday Visitor** / 200 Noll Plaza / Huntington, IN 46750.

- -

Please send me ___ A catalog
Please send me materials on:
___ Apologetics and catechetics
___ Prayer books
___ The family
___ Reference works
___ Heritage and the saints
___ The parish

Name _____
Address _____ Apt._____
City _____ State _____ Zip_____
Telephone (   ) _____

A89BBBBP

- -

Please send a friend ___ A catalog
Please send a friend materials on:
___ Apologetics and catechetics
___ Prayer books
___ The family
___ Reference works
___ Heritage and the saints
___ The parish

Name _____
Address _____ Apt._____
City _____ State _____ Zip_____
Telephone (   ) _____

A89BBBBP

OurSundayVisitor

Bringing Your Catholic Faith to Life
www.osv.com